FIGHT BACK WITH JOY

CELEBRATE MORE. REGRET LESS.
STARE DOWN YOUR GREATEST FEARS.

Margaret Feinberg

CRITICALLY ACCLAIMED AUTHOR OF *WONDERSTRUCK*

Published by LifeWay Press®

ISBN: 9781430038221

Item: 005699445

Dewey Decimal Classification Number: 152.4

Subject Headings: JOY AND SORROW \ FEAR \ CHRISTIAN LIFE

To order additional copies of this resource, write LifeWay Christian Resources Customer Service; One LifeWay Plaza; Nashville, TN 37234-0113; fax order to 615.251.5933; call toll-free 800.459.2772; email *orderentry@lifeway.com;* order online at *www.lifeway.com;* or visit the LifeWay Christian Store serving you.

Printed in the United States of America

Adult Ministry Publishing

LifeWay Church Resources

One LifeWay Plaza

Nashville, Tennessee 37234-0152

TABLE OF CONTENTS

MARGARET FEINBERG

A self-described "hot mess," Margaret Feinberg is a popular Bible teacher at churches and leading conferences such as Catalyst, Thrive, and Women of Joy. She was recently named one of the 50 women most shaping the church and culture by *Christianity Today* and one of the "30 Voices" who will help lead the church in the next decade. Her books, including *The Organic God, The Sacred Echo, Scouting the Divine,* and *Wonderstruck,* as well as their corresponding Bible studies have sold nearly a million copies and have received extensive national media coverage from CNN, *Washington Post,* and *USA Today.* She lives in Morrison, Colorado, with her husband, Leif, and their superpup, Hershey. She believes some of the best days are spent in her jammies, laughing, and being silly.

Now that you've read the official bio, here's the kick off your shoes and drink iced tea on the back porch version:

Margaret spends most mornings with her good friends coffee and God. Without coffee, mornings would be difficult. Without God, life would be impossible.

You'll often find Margaret (puppy-in-tow) adventuring outdoors—she enjoys hiking, river rafting, and scanning the night sky for the Northern Lights and shooting stars.

She boasts an exceptionally dry sense of humor that she attributes to her Jewish father. Little known secret: he was recently inducted into the Surfer's Hall of Fame, and her mom earned her captain's license for 60-ton ships.

Married to Leif for more than a decade, Margaret's known for losing things like her sunglasses on her head, keys in her hand, and her phone for the 12th time in the same day. Always up for an adventure, Margaret is known to drive 50 miles to chase down a food truck and snag Groupons for river rafting on a whim. She prefers watching comedies and laughing until her tummy aches to doing sit ups.

One of her greatest joys is hearing from her readers. So, become her friend on Facebook. Follow her on Twitter or Instagram @mafeinberg. Check out her website at *www.margaretfeinberg.com.*

DEAR GROUP MEMBER,

SEVERAL YEARS AGO I felt compelled by the Holy Spirit to go on a personal journey to lay hold of more joy in my life. I dug into Scripture, researching the hundreds of passages on joy, happiness, rejoicing, merriment, and more.

Thrilled about all I was learning, I was putting the finishing touches on a book when I received the news of a difficult diagnosis. Plunged into a world of greater pain and suffering than I'd ever known, I had to scrap the project. Up until then, I had been searching for joy in the relatively good times of life, now I had to find joy amidst darkness and agony.

No one signs up for that assignment. No one.

Against all odds, I've found my capacity for joy expanding, and I've discovered something quite startling:

Joy is far more than I ever thought or had been taught. It's a more dynamic, forceful weapon than most of us realize. When we fight back with joy, we lean into the very presence of God—the One who fill us with joy, even on our most deflated days.

The prophet Isaiah alludes to such a mysterious discovery when he declares God's promise in Isaiah 45:3 (HCSB[1]), "I will give you the treasures of darkness and riches from secret places, so that you may know that I, Yahweh, the God of Israel call you by your name." And what God promised to Cyrus years ago is true for us, too.

No matter who you are or what your situation—whether your life is marked by cloudless skies and serene seas or a torrential downpour and darkness—I believe God through the power of the Holy Spirit will do a robust work in your life through this study.

Nothing I've ever written has cost me more. My name, Margaret, means *pearl*, one who is shaped by adversity to reflect the glory of God.

My hope and prayer is that this book and Bible study do just that. May the Lord be glorified in my weakness. May you be drawn closer to Jesus. May you find yourself in awe of God's goodness no matter what you're facing.

I love you. I'm praying for you. It's a privilege to study the Bible alongside you. Thank you for joining me to fight back with joy.

Much love,
Margaret

DEAR LEADER,

I AM SO GRATEFUL FOR YOU! I wish I were with you right now to give you a huge hug and whisper thank you in your ear. Thank you for taking the time to lead participants through this book and Bible study called *Fight Back With Joy*. You are busy. Your time is precious and limited. You're pulled in many different directions. Yet here you are willing to step out in faith and courageously serve others as they grow closer to Christ. I give God thanks for you. And I can't wait to hear how He awakens you to the joyful, playful side of His character in the weeks ahead.

Know that our team, my hubby Leif, and I have all been praying for you. We've asked God to speak to you, guide you, encourage you, and equip you. We're praying that the great Joy-Giver, our amazing God, will show up in your gatherings, unleash His transforming power through the homework, and flood each participant's heart until they can't help but frolic in His presence.

I've also asked God that your joy reservoirs will overflow, too, and that as you pour out, you'll find yourself splashing in God's goodness. Drop us a note at *joy@margaretfeinberg.com* and let us know when your group is meeting. We want to pray for you and your participants during this time.

Thank you, sweet friend, for being courageous enough to lead others deeper in their relationship with Jesus. I can't wait to meet you and give you that big hug in person. May you be filled with joy and equipped to fight back with joy because you know beyond a shadow of doubt the battle has already been won.

Blessings,
Margaret

P. S. The book *Fight Back With Joy* is not required for participation in this Bible study, but you may want to recommend group members pick up an electronic, audio, or paperback copy to get the most out of the experience. This is especially true for those facing a crisis of their own, whether that's a diagnosis similar to Margaret's or something completely different.

LEADER'S GUIDE

THIS BRIEF LEADER'S GUIDE is designed to help you take participants through the *Fight Back With Joy* book and Bible study. As you prepare for this study, go ahead and watch several of the video sessions ahead of time so that you'll have a feel for the study's direction.

In the Leader's Kit, you'll find a copy of the *Fight Back With Joy* book. Reading the book in advance will prepare you for leading the study and provide you with additional insights and background. The book is not required for participants, but you may want to recommend group members pick up an electronic, audio, or paperback copy to get the most out of their experience.

As you prepare for each session, here's a basic outline of what to expect:

⤴ EXPERIENTIAL ACTIVITY

Depending on the amount of time you have to meet together and the resources available, you'll want to begin the session with the experiential activity. You will find these activities on the group page that begins each session. This interactive icebreaker is designed to be a trigger for group engagement and help move people toward the ideas explored in the teaching. You'll always want to read ahead to the following week's activity to see what's needed and how participants may be able to contribute.

💬 HOMEWORK GROUP DISCUSSION

Next in each session (with the exception of the first and last) you will lead the group to review the homework from the previous session. Encourage participants to share what they're learning and how the Holy Spirit is at work in their lives.

▶ PLAY SESSION VIDEO

After you've finished the homework discussion, it's time to play the video. The teaching presentations will range from 20-30 minutes.

66 NOTES

Each notes page includes key statements from that week's teaching. Encourage participants to fill in the blanks and jot down notes, questions, and details as they watch the video.

💬 VIDEO DISCUSSION

Dive into the video discussion questions next. Based on the amount of time your group meets, you may need to prayerfully consider which questions are best suited for your group and their needs. Don't feel as though you need to ask every question. Rely on the Holy Spirit for guidance on any additional questions or follow-up that needs to be asked as the discussion progresses.

💜 CLOSING PRAYER

Always save time for prayer before you close. Ask the Holy Spirit to open everyone's eyes and hearts to receive the gift of joy in greater measure.

Thank you, again, for leading this Bible study. I pray that you begin experiencing the joy of God in fresh, new ways.

SECRETS OF JOYFUL PEOPLE

GROUP GETTING STARTED: (10-15 minutes)

SESSION ONE:
SECRETS OF JOYFUL PEOPLE

✦ EXPERIENTIAL ACTIVITY: BUILD A PARTY HAT

WHAT YOU'LL NEED:

- Several sheets of colored paper for each person
- Assorted stickers
- Markers
- Tape
- A stapler
- Ribbon

1 Invite each person to decorate a party hat. The design can take any shape or form, so invite participants to be wildly creative. Use ribbon to accent or to create a tie to keep the hat atop the head. Add stickers. Use colors to embellish.

2 Write words or draw pictures of things that bring joy. This can include anything: people in their lives, encouraging words, activities, memories, gifts, interactions. Ask participants to cover their party hats with sources of joy. When they've completed their hats, ask them to place them atop their heads.

3 Discuss the following:

   Briefly share what was drawn or written on each hat.

   Where are some of the places you've looked for joy and found it?
   Where are some of the places you've looked for joy and not found it?

   Reflect on what everyone shared. What are some of the most common sources of joy among the group?

▶ **PLAY THE SESSION ONE VIDEO:** [18:25]

Follow along with Margaret and fill in the blanks for each statement below. Take additional notes in the space provided when you hear something that resonates with you.

Joy emanates out of the abiding sense of _God's fierce love for us_

Tactic 1. Marinate in the truth of _God's_ _fierce_ _love_ _for_ _you_.

    I John 3:1

    Jer. 31:3

    Isai 54:10

    Isaiah 43:4

    Zeph. 3:17

Am I loved?
Does it matter that I exist?
God loves me

Tactic 2. Live on high alert that _God_ _is_ _here_.

Joy bombs

Tactic 3. Bravely believe _God_ _is_ _for_ _you_. (me)

Luke 12:32

Fear not, little flock for your father has been pleased to give you the kingdom.

▶ VIDEO DISCUSSION

1 Turn to page 168. Over the next six weeks, we're asking God to expand our capacity to experience joy. One of the ways to do this is to make daily entries in the Joy Bomb Journal. Begin today by listing three joy bombs in your life. Consider sharing with the group if your responses are different from the experiential activity.

2 I list some of the less than desirable declarations I had been making in my life. What declarations have you been unintentionally making with your life?

3 Invite someone to read John 15:11 aloud. When was the last time you prayed for God to give you more joy? What prevents you from praying for joy more often?

4 When you look at Scripture, *joy* is "a spectrum of emotions, actions, and responses that include gladness, cheer, happiness, merriment, delighting, dancing, shouting, exulting, rejoicing, laughing, playing, brightening, blessing and being blessed, taking pleasure in, and being well pleased." Which among these come most naturally to you? Which are more difficult?

5 Joy emanates out of the abiding sense of God's fierce love for us. On a scale of 1-10, how much joy do you have right now? On a scale of 1-10, how would you rate your awareness of God's fierce love for you? Do you see any connection? Why or why not?

6 In what situation in your life do you most need to say, "God loves me. God is here. God is for me."?

♥ CLOSING PRAYER

As you close in prayer ask:

- God to expand each participant's capacity for joy;
- the Holy Spirit to awaken a deep sense of God's fierce love;
- that each participant would be able to recognize and joyfully receive all the good gifts God gives each day.

happy vs. Joy

AWAKEN TO GOD'S FIERCE LOVE

✎ THIS WEEK:

If you're following along in the book, read chapters ".000 Why We Live Joyless Lives" and ".001 A Choice That Changed Everything" and dive into the five days of homework to prepare for the next gathering.

"How much joy do you have in your life?"

The abrupt question caught me off guard. If someone, anyone, but my long-time friend, Olivia, had asked I would have recoiled, but even her most penetrating questions are always bubble-wrapped in so much love.

My index finger took a few spins around the thick edge of my empty coffee mug as I thought of my response. Possibilities waved about like a broken sprinkler head.

Glancing up at Olivia's tender eyes, I knew she'd wait as long as needed for an answer, a characteristic that made me adore our friendship all the more.

My eyes fluttered about the café in search of an honest answer.

"On a scale of 1 to 10, I'm a 3," I confessed.

"Why do you think it's such a low score?" she probed.

📖 NOTABLE:

Filming for *Fight Back With Joy* video sessions took place in a lovely rented home in Nashville, Tennessee.

Reasons flickered in my mind and started flowing like melted wax. "Some days I feel isolated. Others I am discouraged too easily. I feel restless and stuck."

Olivia reflected so much grace in her response.

"Joy is a gift God wants to expand in your life," she said. "You can be more joyful tomorrow than you are today."

Her words echoed deep and true inside me:

"Joy is a gift."

"You can be more joyful tomorrow than you are today."

As we begin, I want to tenderly look in your eyes and ask the same question Olivia asked me:

> How much joy do you have in your life? On a scale of 1 to 10, how would you rate your level of joy today? (Circle) the number below.

1   2   3   4   (5)   (6)   7   8   9   10

Sometimes it's hard to be honest with ourselves. When I said the number 3 aloud, my face scrunched. No one wants to be a 3. I'd much rather be an 11! Or 12!

But I had to make a candid assessment of where I was before I could journey to where God wanted me to be.

Thanks to Olivia and her gentle prodding, along with a few other *sacred echoes,* I began a journey to lay hold of a deeper, more abundant joy than I had ever experienced before.

Until then, I believed joy would naturally flourish in my life without any effort or work. Somehow joy would abound with each passing day. But if anything, my joy was slipping away.

As I began to explore joy, I soon recognized the close connection between love and joy. Whenever love walks in the room, joy is close behind. If love brings chips, then joy adds guacamole. They travel together, camp together, have sleepovers together. The reason we can experience joy is because of God's fierce love. Joy flows out of God's affection for us. That's why I'm convinced:

JOY EMANATES OUT OF THE ABIDING SENSE OF GOD'S FIERCE LOVE FOR US.

One of the foundational ways we can begin to grow in joy is by spending time grounding ourselves in the truth of God's tremendous love for us. We need to spelunk the depths, probe the widths, and scale the heights of His affection for us. This is the surest path to joy.

GOD'S FIERCE LOVE ⟶ JOY

My hunch is that you desire God's love to break into your life in a fresh, vibrant way, too. Perhaps, like me, you ache for the uncontainable love of God to fill you, saturate you, and overflow in such a way that it drips out of you everywhere you go. When you have that abiding sense of God's fierce love—a love that will

NOTABLE:

A sacred echo is the repetitive nature of God's voice in your life. Often when God speaks, He will say the same thing again and again. See 1 Kings 19.

carry you through every circumstance, challenge, and battle you face—you can't help but experience more joy.

For me, Psalm 90:14 (NIV[1]) has become a personal prayer: "Satisfy us in the morning with your unfailing love, that we may sing for joy and be glad all our days." This verse even sparked a spiritual discipline of sorts. I began spending time each morning reading over Scripture that grounded me in the wild affection of God. I rummaged through translations that used the most vibrant, passionate, soul-stirring language to describe God's affection and collected a list of verses about God's love. In the deepest parts of my soul, I needed to awaken to the fierce love of my Heavenly Father.

Below are a handful of passages that whispered hope into the depths of my spirit, courage into the recesses of my heart, and deep joy into my weary bones.

Will you take a few minutes each day this week to read through the following passages? Even as you're moving onto other homework lessons, dog-ear this page and ground yourself in the truth of God's fierce love for you again and again.

Before you read, ask the Holy Spirit to awaken a deeper sense of God's affection for you. As you read, add your name in the underlined spaces. Circle key phrases. ✳Star meaningful words. Place the date by any passage you sense God is specifically speaking to you on a particular day. Consider committing a few or all to memory.

➕ BONUS ACTIVITY:

Spend time committing Psalm 16:11 to memory this week. You'll find a flash card on page 193.

I've never quit loving you, _____Sandra_____ and never will. Expect love, love, and more love!

JEREMIAH 31:3, MSG[2]

The mountains and hills may crumble, but my love for you, _____Sandra_____, will never end.

ISAIAH 54:10, GNT[3]

I paid a huge price for you, _____Sandra_____ ...
That's how much you mean to me! That's how much I love you! I'd sell off the whole world to get you back, trade the creation just for you.

ISAIAH 43:4, MSG

The LORD your God is with you; the mighty One will save you.

He will rejoice over you. You, ___*Sandra*___ will rest in his love; he will sing and be joyful about you.

ZEPHANIAH 3:17, NCV[4]

But you, O Lord, are a God of compassion and mercy, slow to get angry and filled with unfailing love and faithfulness for ___*Sandra*___.

PSALM 86:15, NLT[5]

GOD's loyal love couldn't have run out, his merciful love for ___*Sandra*___ couldn't have dried up. They're created new every morning.

LAMENTATIONS 3:22, MSG

But God demonstrates his own love for ___*Sandra*___ in this: While we were still sinners, Christ died for us.

ROMANS 5:8, NIV

What marvelous love the Father has extended to ___*Sandra*___! Just look at it—we're called children of God!

1 JOHN 3:1, MSG

I've loved you, ___*Sandra*___, the way my Father has loved me. Make yourselves at home in my love.

JOHN 15:9, MSG

 QUOTABLE:

"No man truly has joy unless he lives in love." —Thomas Aquinas, Italian priest[6]

 **BONUS ACTIVITY:**

If you'd like to see the full Scripture list that Margaret used, email *joy@margaretfeinberg.com*.

No matter how joyful you are today, God has even more joy waiting for you. My hope and prayer is that through this first week of homework, you'll ground yourself in the fierce love of God. With each passing day, may you become more intentional about choosing joy, pursuing joy, and activating joy in your life.

CLOSING PRAYER: Spend time asking God to expand your capacity to experience His joy. With each passing page and session, ask God to deepen the abiding sense of His fierce love for you.

ORIGINATED IN GOD, DEMONSTRATED IN CHRIST

The tiny fingers of a newborn clutch onto the tip of your pinky. Generations of friends and family gather around. A child in black tap shoes, three sizes too big, dances with wild abandon, bringing back memories of when you used to frolic that way. Plates of roasted chicken with steamed vegetables are savored alongside loved ones in God's living room under the stars. Cheeks ache from too much sidesplitting laughter. When you tuck yourself in bed, you know you've truly lived.

These are the moments when the soul seems to breathe, when blood returns to our white-knuckled lives, when we begin to dream that such moments aren't exceptions but meant to surge through our everyday.

What water is to parched lips, joy is to the spirit.

Circle the items below that bring you joy:

- **Yummy food**
- **Hanging with friends**
- **Spending time with family**
- **Checking items off your to-do list**
- **Praying**
- **Decorating your house**
- **Planning a party**

- **Exercising**
- **Spending time outdoors**
- **Studying the Bible**
- **A good night's sleep**
- **Giving a gift**
- **A hug from someone you love**
- **Other:**

+ BONUS ACTIVITY:

Remember, joy emanates out of the abiding sense of God's fierce love for you. As you start today's lesson, will you take a few minutes to read through the passages found in Day One that speak of God's fierce love for you?

My friend, Troy, has a daughter who is a 6-year-old ball of hilarity. She's constantly cackling with delight. One night at bedtime, Troy remembers her praying:

"God, tomorrow may we have gladness and get the energy up."

Troy's first thought was, *Who prays like that?*

Perhaps we all should.

In her beautiful, 6-year-old way, this precious child was praying for more joy.

She was asking God to shower her family with more cheer and vitality. Troy wasn't the only one smiling at his daughter's prayer. I suspect God was, too.

When was the last time you prayed for God to give you more joy?

not sure I ever have

If you're like me, you may be hesitant to pray for joy, because, well, it can feel a little self-indulgent. Most of us wouldn't think twice about praying to become more holy or righteous, but asking for joy can feel hedonistic. Yet I believe God takes delight when we abound in joy, because He is the source of all joy.

> In thy presence is fulness of joy; at thy right
> hand there are pleasures for evermore."
> **PSALM 16:11, KJV**[7]

In whom and where is joy found according to this passage?

The LORD

In alluding to God's right hand, the author is anthropomorphizing God (giving Him human-like characteristics). The right hand signifies power throughout Scripture. Jesus is seated at God's right hand (see Col. 3:1; Acts 2:33). True joy and pleasure are found in Christ.

The psalmists reveal that the quest for joy is not just an option made available to us but something we are commanded to pursue.

What is the condition of receiving the desires of your heart according to Psalm 37:4?

Delighting yourself in the Lord

What is the longing expressed in Psalm 63:1?

Our body longs for God.

How is this longing fulfilled in Psalm 36:8?

we are able to drink from the River of delights

Do you see the heart cry of the psalmists? We are called to seek and obey God, but we are also called to enjoy God and partake in the most satisfying pleasure imaginable—a joy that can only be found in Him. We are meant to live in such a way that God's pleasure becomes second nature. Indeed, joy is the hearty echo of God's great love for us.

When we find our joy in God, we bring Him glory. That's a fancy-pants, theological way of saying that every day you walk in joy, you put a smile on your Heavenly Papa's face.

God is so wildly generous with His joy that He doesn't keep it all to Himself. He desires to share it with us. God wants His joy to become our joy.

In fact, an abundance of joy is a powerful witness to the beauty of a relationship with God.

NOTABLE:

The Old Testament teaches us that joy stems from God the Father (see Isa. 9:3). Jesus connects Himself to the same virtue in John 15:11 using possessive language. He says "My" joy, not "joy like mine." Paul speaks of joy in Galatians 5 as a fruit of the Spirit. The fact that joy is tied to all three persons of the Trinity underscores its importance in the life of a Christian.

Perhaps the greatest demonstration of the joy God wants to share with us is found in the person of Jesus Christ.

God's only Son crashed into our world with an angel broadcasting,

> "I bring you good news that will cause great joy for all the people."
> LUKE 2:10, NIV

Before leaving our world, Jesus endowed the disciples with the promise:

> "These things I have spoken to you so that My joy may
> be in you, and that your joy may be made full."
> JOHN 15:11, NASB[8]

Jesus arrives in joy, departs in joy, and calls us to great joy through unbroken fellowship with Him. The gospel is an invitation to experience more of God's joy in our lives—not just when we get to heaven, but beginning here, now, today.

Pause and ask God to increase your desire and capacity to experience more of the joy that He wants to give you. Write your prayer below.

Dear Heavenly Papa …

Help me to experience the Joy you have intended for me. Give me the boldness to ask for it everyday + the energy to enjoy it. Amen

(verb) manifest: to make clear or evident. show plainly; to prove; put beyond doubt;

You and I are called to a life marked by gladness (see Ps. 67:4), rejoicing (see Phil. 4:4), blessedness (see Jer. 17:7), happiness (see Ps. 146:5), and much, much more! As children of God, we are meant to radiate God's joy and leave a well-littered trail of divine affection and delight wherever we go.

WE ARE MEANT TO DO MORE THAN MIMIC JESUS; WE ARE TO MANIFEST HIM.

Do you tend to mimic Jesus or manifest Him wherever you go? Which do you think will have a more long-lasting impact? Explain.

manifest. prove his love by loving like him.

My hope and prayer is that your heart will awaken anew to the pleasure that is originated in God and demonstrated in Christ. And that you will become a disciple of Jesus whose life is marked by the joyfulness and playfulness of your Heavenly Father rather than drudgery or duty.

♥ **CLOSING PRAYER:** Spend time thanking God for His abundant joy. Give thanks for the generosity He showed you in sending His Son, Jesus. Ask Him to help you manifest Christ's joy wherever you go today.

CELEBRATE THE BEAUTIFUL SPECTRUM OF JOY

A few years ago, Leif and I needed to purchase a vehicle. For most people, purchasing a car is straightforward. But when your best friend and hubby is 6'8", the process becomes much more complex—especially when you're looking for a fuel efficient, smaller vehicle.

Captain Tall, as I like to call him, scrunched into more than one hundred cars. He attended the Denver Auto Show and spent countless Saturdays with friends visiting dealerships and used car lots. In the end, our decision boiled down to either a Smart Car or a Volkswagen. Believe it or not, he fit in both!

We chose the Volkswagen.

Now something strange happened once we purchased our first Volkswagen.

💬 **QUOTABLE:**

"The infinite happiness of the Father consists in the enjoyment of His Son." —Jonathan Edwards, theologian[9]

💬 **QUOTABLE:**

"We want to pull a lever and see the world change. Political involvement is not the issue; the joy of God is the issue. Remember, the joy of God is the state of flourishing in mind, heart, and life that Christians experience by the Holy Spirit. We've been so anxious to influence society in the past century that we've ended up going after a lot of shortcuts. For some it's politics, for some it's education, for some it's evangelism. We've been pulling a lot of levers. The common thread is that we're pulling these levers so hard, we leave no space for people to encounter the joy of God." —Dr. Greg Forster, Director of the Kern Family Foundation[10]

Maybe you've experienced it. Every time we drove on the highway, Volkswagens surrounded us. Every parking lot overflowed with them. We'd never seen so many Volkswagens in our lives. These cars were everywhere!

Describe a time you had something like this happen to you.

Someone you've never seen before suddenly you see everywhere

Psychologists describe this as the Baader-Meinhof Phenomenon. It occurs whenever a word, name, or item that has come to your attention seems to appear in high frequency.

Perhaps I shouldn't have been surprised that when I started choosing, pursuing, and activating joy, the word appeared everywhere—especially when I read the Bible. Little references to joy I'd never noticed before began popping off pages.

Just this morning, I sat wonderstruck by the "thousands upon thousands of angels in joyful assembly" described in Hebrews 12:22 (NIV). What a holy ruckus! Can you imagine the singing, dancing, exulting, and playfulness in this heavenly scene?

Joy didn't just zing as I read the Bible; those three letters appeared at the mall, in my favorite coffee shop, even on television ads. Joy is everywhere—on coffee mugs, t-shirts, home décor—even on my dish soap.

Where have you seen the word *joy* pop up since you started this Bible study?

Same type of places Stamps, T-shirts, plaques - hobby lobby

What I've been observing, and maybe you've noticed it too, is that our culture seems to be confused about joy. It's one of those words that has been hijacked by marketers, overused, and even transformed into a cliché.

When I'm curious about what our culture thinks of something specific, I search the word or idea on Google images. This afternoon, I typed in the word *joy*. Two primary images popped up. First, the word *joy* appeared in all kinds of colorful designs including some yummy looking cookies.

The second type of image was people mid-leap as if they were in one of those old Toyota commercials where a person jumps and shouts "Toy-ota!"

I chuckled.

NOTABLE:

Q: Why didn't Noah go fishing?
A: He only had two worms.

Q: How does Moses make his coffee?
A: Hebrews it.

Q: How do we know Peter was a rich fisherman?
A: By his net income.

The Joy of the Lord is my Strength. Nehemiah 8:10

Our culture associates joy with the word *joy* (which isn't helpful) as well as an impossible-to-maintain bounciness.

How would you define joy?

happiness

How do you think culture has influenced your definition?

Joy is associated with sunlight jumping for joy, Serenity

Over the last few years, as I've dug into Scripture, I've become convinced that God wants to give us a richer, deeper, fuller understanding of joy than we realize. The joy God has for us is grander than any single emotion, action, or response.

To embrace the fullness of joy that God has for us, we need to broaden, rather than narrow, our understanding of joy. When you look at Scripture:

JOY INVOLVES A SPECTRUM OF EMOTIONS, ACTIONS, AND RESPONSES THAT INCLUDE GLADNESS, CHEER, HAPPINESS, MERRIMENT, DELIGHTING, DANCING, SHOUTING, EXULTING, REJOICING, LAUGHING, PLAYING, BRIGHTENING, BLESSING AND BEING BLESSED, TAKING PLEASURE IN, AND BEING WELL-PLEASED.

Each of these expressions is rooted in Scripture—either in God's response to His creation (including us) or our response to God. Much like a spectrum of colors, joy is varied and beautiful. Some joys are expressed verbally; others are nonverbal. Some joys are visible to the eye; others are invisible but still profound, real, and transformative.

Our response to the joy God gives may be loud and include laughter, shouting (also known as whooping it up!), and rejoicing. Or it may be more subdued and include the brightening of the face, the deep sense of being blessed, and the pleasure found in being God's beloved child.

WHAT DOES JOY LOOK LIKE?

QUOTABLE:

"I believe what God has in mind, and what the Bible really says, is that joy is a real emotion. God commands us to feel happy, feel joy, feel good. To feel the real emotions of joy. Not all the time, of course, not in every season or at every moment—God is not interested in plastic Christians. But somehow, the good feeling of joy should be something that defines who we are. We should be people who live in this place of real, emotional joy. What God has in mind is not a redefinition of joy, but a redefinition of us." —Matthew Elliot, writer and theologian[11]

Underline the different expressions of joy found in each of the following passages. Then (circle) the words that best describe the expression, whether it's verbal or nonverbal, visible or invisible. Note that some passages may have more than one joyful expression.

Example:

Shout for joy to the LORD, all the earth.

PSALM 100:1, NIV

(Verbal) or Nonverbal   Visible or (Invisible)

Then you will look and be radiant, your heart will throb and (swell with joy), the wealth on the seas will be brought to you, to you the riches of the nations will come.

ISAIAH 60:5, NIV

Verbal or (Nonverbal)   Visible or (Invisible)

Then Leah said, "How happy I am! The women will call me happy." So she named him Asher.

GENESIS 30:13, NIV

(Verbal or Nonverbal)   (Visible) or Invisible

Your statutes are my delight; they are my counselors.

PSALM 119:24, NIV

Verbal or (Nonverbal)   Visible or (Invisible)

But let the righteous be glad; let them exult before God; Yes, let them rejoice with gladness.

PSALM 68:3, NASB

Verbal or (Nonverbal)   Visible or (Invisible)

Those who look to Him are radiant with joy; their faces will never be ashamed.

PSALM 34:5, HCSB

Verbal or (Nonverbal)   (Visible) or Invisible

Surely you have granted him unending blessings and made him glad with the joy of your presence.

PSALM 21:6, NIV

Verbal or (Nonverbal)   (Visible) or Invisible

QUOTABLE:

"Joy and laughter are the gifts of living in the presence of God and trusting that tomorrow is not worth worrying about." —Henri Nouwen, author[12]

All the days of the oppressed are wretched,
but the cheerful heart has a continual feast.
PROVERBS 15:15, NIV
Verbal or (Nonverbal)   **Visible or (Invisible)**

"Again I will build you and you will be rebuilt,
O virgin of Israel!
Again you will take up your tambourines,
And go forth to the dances of the merrymakers."
JEREMIAH 31:4, NASB
(Verbal) or Nonverbal   **(Visible) or Invisible**

When the LORD brought back the captive ones of Zion,
we were like those who dream.
Then our mouth was filled with laughter;
and our tongue with joyful shouting;
Then they said among the nations,
"The LORD has done great things for them."
The LORD has done great things for us;
We are glad.
PSALM 126:1-3, NASB
(Verbal) or Nonverbal   **(Visible) or Invisible**

But we had to celebrate and be glad, because this brother of
yours was dead and is alive again; he was lost and is found.
LUKE 15:32, NIV
Verbal or (Nonverbal)   **Visible or (Invisible)**

The LORD takes pleasure in those who fear him,
in those who hope in his steadfast love.
PSALM 147:11, ESV[13]
Verbal or (Nonverbal)   **Visible or (Invisible)**

> **NOTABLE:**
>
> Throughout the Old Testament we see the Hebrew word *asher* used to describe a person who is pronounced "happy" or "blessed." This word is often used within the context of the flourishing of God's people: "Happy is that people, that is in such a case: yea, happy is that people, whose God is the LORD" (Ps. 144:15, KJV).

Throughout this study, we're going to look at many passages about joy, but I wanted to give you a bird's-eye view of some expressions of joy. Why? Because broadening your understanding of joy will expand your capacity to experience joy.

Reflecting on these Scriptures, maybe you realize it's been far too long since you shouted for joy, threw a celebration, picked up a musical instrument (even if it's just a spoon and cooking pan for a homemade drum), or felt your heart swell with holy delight.

Seeing all the different biblical expressions of joy—verbal and nonverbal, visible and invisible—may prompt you to experience some new ones in the weeks ahead.

> **Place a check √ by the expressions of joy that come easily for you.**
> **Place a star ✴ by the expressions of joy that are more challenging.**

❑ Gladness   ❑ Cheer
❑ Happiness   ❑ Merriment
❑ Delighting   ✴ Dancing
✴ Shouting   ❑ Exulting
❑ Rejoicing   ☑ Laughing
☑ Playing   ❑ Brightening
❑ Blessing/being blessed
☑ Taking pleasure in/being well-pleased

QUOTABLE:

"Is anyone happy? Let them sing songs of praise."
—James 5:13, NIV

Growing up in the church, I was taught from a young age that joy is a deep and remaining friend, but happiness was a far more circumstantial acquaintance. Happiness was persnickety about coming to the party of life. If the appetizers weren't fabulous or the right people weren't in the room, then happiness would disappear out the back door like a fickle friend. Happiness wasn't to be trusted or celebrated.

But passages like James 5:13 instruct us that when we are happy, we are to give praise to God. In other words, happiness issues us a holy call to worship. In 2 Corinthians 7:13, we glimpse Paul rejoicing because Titus is happy. These and other verses began challenging my narrow thinking.

I realized I had spent a lot of years thinking I just needed joy and not happiness.

> **Have you ever met someone who is truly joyful and completely unhappy?**

How about someone busting at the seams with happiness but maintaining zero joy?

As children of God, could our circumstances be any better? We have so many reasons to be ebullient. We are drenched in the mercies, grace, and love of God.

I long for all the joy and happiness and blessedness and delight and merriment and celebration that God wants to give me as His child. I want the fullness of the pleasures at God's right hand and the fullness of joy found in Christ.

My hunch is that you do, too.

That's why from time to time we need to do a prayer checkup to see if there are ways we may be neglecting opportunities for greater joy, happiness, and celebration. Here are a few that I've recognized.

Place a check ✓ mark beside those you can relate to:

- ☑ I allow myself to be too busy.
- ☑ I focus more on tasks than people.
- ☑ I say no to an invitation to a dinner party or celebration.
- ☑ I hold back from making time to sing and praise.
- ☑ I resist making space for new people in my life.
- ❏ I allow pain and discouragement to shape my responses.
- ❏ I settle for that which would make me feel better rather than my best.

Will you take a moment to ask God to reveal any places in your heart where you've said no to joy, happiness, or celebration?

Show me where I am missing out on joy + happiness

Let's make a commitment together that we will seek God for all the ways He wants to fill us with joy, happiness, and delight. That we will be people whose lives are marked by celebration because we're loved fiercely by God.

💙 **CLOSING PRAYER:** Continue to ask God to reveal any areas where you're missing out on the fullness of joy that He wants to give you. Ask Him to supernaturally allow you to experience more of His joy than you've ever experienced before.

UNWRAP CREATIONAL AND REDEMPTIVE GIFTS

Let's start this lesson with The Good Gift Giver Quiz.

Select the answers that best describe you:

The gifts you most love giving are:
A. Highly personal and packaged in themed wrapping paper with a matching ribbon and card;
B. A blend of fun and practical;
C. Always accompanied by the receipt so the person can return it if he or she doesn't like or need it.

You are most likely to do your Christmas shopping:
A. Throughout the year when you find the perfect items;
B. Any time after Black Friday;
C. Online two weeks before Christmas.

The most common response when someone unwraps your gift is:
A. "Wow! You really know me."
B. "Ha-ha—you're funny."
C. "That's exactly what I needed."

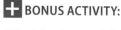 **BONUS ACTIVITY:**

Gift giving is one of the five love languages as described in *The Five Love Languages* by Gary D. Chapman. This is a great resource for people of all ages.

If you answered mostly A's, you're an extravagant gifter. You love to go over the top and express your affection for others through the presents you select and give.

If you answered mostly B's, you're a generous gifter. You love to think about what people need, but you also want to bring a smile to their face when they open the gift.

If you answered mostly C's, you're a thoughtful gifter. You love to use gifts as opportunities to meet real needs and make sure people receive what they'd like and enjoy.

Which kind of gifter are you? What are your favorite kinds of gifts to receive?

B- generous gifter. I like giving crafty gifts or something more exciting than practical.

What kind of connections exist between the gifts you enjoy receiving and the gifts you enjoy giving?

Very similar, I like craft gifts unique items

All of us have different styles in the way we select, wrap, and give gifts. I tend to be more of a thoughtful gifter. I try to include the gift receipts so the item can be returned. To me, gift cards aren't impersonal, but a way to ensure friends receive their absolute favorite items. Most of my gifts look like a 9-year-old wrapped them. That's why I tend to stick to gift bags and tissue paper or, when possible, ask the store to gift wrap for me.

Though my gifts are humble and imperfect offerings, they are signs of my love and affection. Like most gifts, they are given with the hope that the item, or the thoughtfulness behind the item, will bring comfort, delight, and joy.

When it comes to giving good gifts, no one is more extraordinary or extravagant than God. James 1:17 (NIV) tells us:

> Every good and perfect gift is from above, coming
> down from the Father of the heavenly lights, who
> does not change like shifting shadows.

Every. Last. One.

WHEN IT COMES TO DOLING OUT HAPPINESS AND JOY, GOD IS ANYTHING BUT STINGY.

Unlike our gifts, which are sometimes imperfect or ill-timed, all of God's gifts are jam-packed with His goodness and stamped with perfection. Our God is so generous that He gives good gifts to all of humanity. These are called *creational gifts* because they are part of every human life. Each one of these joy bombs has the capacity to generate joy and happiness.

In the following passages, circle the creational gifts of God that bring joy and happiness. Note that some passages will mention more than one good gift of God.

> He causes the grass to grow for the cattle,
> And vegetation for the labor of man,
> So that he may bring forth food from the earth,
> And wine which makes man's heart glad,

So that he may make his face glisten with oil,
*—And (food) which sustains man's heart.
PSALM 104:14-15, NASB

He gives the childless woman (a family,)
making her a happy mother.
PSALM 113:9, NLT

*(Children) are a gift from the LORD.
PSALM 127:3, NLT

*
An encouraging (word) cheers a person up.
PROVERBS 12:25, NLT

And people should eat and drink and enjoy the
*(fruits) of their labor, for these are gifts from God.
ECCLESIASTES 3:13, NLT

You will enlarge the nation of Israel, and its people will
rejoice. They will rejoice before you as people rejoice at
the (harvest) and like warriors dividing the plunder.
ISAIAH 9:3, NLT

✚ BONUS ACTIVITY:
Some of God's more
unusual creational gifts
are still being discovered
today. Check out the
Smithsonian National
Museum of Natural
History's Ocean Portal
online to see photos
of mysterious and
spectacular deep sea
creatures. Visit *www.
ocean.si.edu/deep-sea.*

Now go back through this verse and place a star ✳ by each of these
wondrous creational gifts of God that you've experienced.

In addition to the encouraging words of others, delicious meals with friends,
and delight of seeing kids play on a lazy Saturday, I've experienced countless
creational gifts of God. Joy bombs are going off all over the place.

Right now I'm watching the radiant splash of colors as the sun casts its last
rays and dips below the horizon. A cool sip of water refreshes my parched
lips. I take my next breath. Every moment I'm experiencing the richness of
the creational gifts of God.

What are three creational gifts of God you're experiencing right now?

1. A great temperature day
2. light to read by
3. my family surrounding me.

What are three of your favorite creational gifts of God?

1. *Children*
2. *the beauty of the outdoors, views, mountains, beaches*
3. *love of others*

Four of my all-time favorite creation gifts include the gift of belly laughter, a strong cup of morning coffee, the hush of an empty walking trail, and the cuddle of a pup. God fashioned all these for which I'm mighty grateful.

Some Christians like to say they're the only ones who have experienced true joy. Not only do such statements make believers sound arrogant and judgmental, but worse, such declarations portray God as stingy with His good gifts. Scripture reveals God as so ridiculously generous that He gives good gifts to *all* people. God throws joy bombs at everyone. This is a living testimony to the goodness, generosity, and love of our Heavenly Father.

That said, as we dig deeper into Scripture we discover those who enter into a relationship with God through His Son, Jesus Christ, are promised a new dimension of life and joy—even more joy bombs. They begin to receive something called *redemptive gifts*.

In the following passages, circle the redemptive gifts of God that bring happiness and joy. Note that some passages will mention more than one good gift of God.

I will exalt you, LORD, for you rescued me.
You refused to let my enemies triumph over me.
O LORD my God, I cried to you for help,
and you restored my health.
You brought me up from the grave, O LORD.
You kept me from falling into the pit of death.
PSALM 30:1-3, NLT

Oh, what joy for those
whose disobedience is forgiven,
whose sin is put out of sight!
PSALM 32:1, NLT

Restore to me the joy of your salvation.
PSALM 51:12, NLT

It's worth noting that a wide variety of God's good gifts have the capacity to generate joy and delight in our lives. Perhaps you also noticed that the gifts often involve relationship with others either directly or implicitly. Joy is often generated as we live life with each other.

Your laws are my treasure;
they are my heart's delight.
PSALM 119:111, NLT

Let all the people of Jerusalem shout his praise with joy!
For great is the Holy One of Israel who lives among you.
ISAIAH 12:6, NLT

When I discovered your words, I devoured them.
They are my joy and my heart's delight,
for I bear your name,
O LORD God of Heaven's Armies.
JEREMIAH 15:16, NLT

Now go back through this list and place a star ✳ by each of these wondrous redemptive gifts of God that you've experienced.

If you've come into a relationship with Jesus Christ, our generous God doesn't just shower you with creational gifts, He pours out redemptive gifts on you as well. You can experience the joy and delight that comes with experiencing salvation, forgiveness, restoration, redemption, God's Word, His presence, and the promise of heaven.

I don't know about you, but I'm bubbling with thanks for the many redemptive gifts of God. As I sit here, I'm so thankful for the grace and mercy that God has shown me over the years. I find comfort and joy in the many promises of God—including His promise that the work He has begun in me He will bring to completion (see Phil. 1:6). I'm appreciative of God's salvation, redemption, goodness … the list could run a mile long.

What are three redemptive gifts of God you've experienced?

1. forgiveness
2. grace
3. salvation

What three redemptive gifts of God are you most thankful for?

1.
2.
3.

I believe that as followers of Jesus we are meant to live palms up, ready to receive God's generosity—both in creational gifts and redemptive gifts—each and every day. We're meant to live wide-eyed for all the joy bombs God is tossing at us. All the while, we know that even the most wondrous gifts are only foretastes of what we will experience when we live in heaven and spend eternity with Him.

How do we begin to unwrap more of these good gifts of God in our lives? I believe we can find guidance in Ecclesiastes 5:18-20 (MSG). Underline any phrases that are particularly helpful to you as you read:

> After looking at the way things are on this earth, here's what I've decided is the best way to live: Take care of yourself, have a good time, and make the most of whatever job you have for as long as God gives you life. And that's about it. That's the human lot. Yes, we should make the most of what God gives, both the bounty and the capacity to enjoy it, accepting what's given and delighting in the work. It's God's gift! God deals out joy in the present, the now. It's useless to brood over how long we might live.

Right now, our joy-giving God is filling our lives with good gifts—presents that are meant to bring joy, delight, and laughter. Some of these gifts are creational. Some are redemptive. All are insignias of God's fierce love for us. Our response should be one of abundant gratitude and obedience to Him.

If we want to experience more joy, then we need to heighten our attention to the gifts our good and generous God is giving us in the midst of every day. We need to spend time each day observing the moments or circumstances where we experience joy. We must pay attention to where we are and whom we're with. When is God tossing joy bombs into our lives and we aren't even noticing?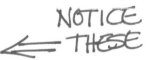

That's why I want you to join me in jotting down your joy discoveries each day. One of the best ways to abound in joy is to keep track of all the good gifts God is giving you.

On page 168, you'll find the Joy Bomb Journal. This is a space where I'm inviting you to write down three things that bring you joy each day. These can be creational gifts like the fiery shades of a sunrise, the tender grip of an infant, or the ability to take one more breath. All are gifts of God.

NOTABLE:

The author of Ecclesiastes believes that life is meaningless unless centered upon God. He uses the word *vanity* 33 times to refer to the emptiness of life if God isn't included, a reminder that every gift we experience comes from God. This call to enjoyment is to turn our eyes to the great Gift-Giver in thanksgiving.

Or perhaps this is a day when you're experiencing a heightened awareness of some of the redemptive gifts of God. Maybe right now you could do a little dance at the thought of being called a child of God. Perhaps you've read a Scripture that breathed life into your weary soul. Or maybe you sense the freedom that comes with asking for forgiveness. All of these are gifts of God, too.

> **Turn to the Joy Bomb Journal and write down at least three things God has given you today that bring you joy. Each of these is an insignia of just how much you are fiercely loved by God. Take a few moments to give thanks to God for each one.**

💙 **CLOSING PRAYER:** Spend time thanking God for being so generous in the good gifts He gives all of humanity and His children. Thank God for being a Joy-Giver.

PRACTICE EVERY DAY JOY

NOTABLE:
God wired your body to benefit from laughter. A good old-fashioned giggle releases chemicals in your brain that equip your body to better handle stress and pain.

Friend, I have to be honest with you. I feel like I've been pushing you hard through this week's homework. Or maybe I've just been pushing myself hard! In this first session, we've covered some major ground.

We've been looking at how many of us don't live in the fullness of joy because we don't understand what joy is, whom it comes from, how much joy is available to us, and where to look for it.

I think it's appropriate to finish off this week with some fun. Let's kick off our shoes, pop some popcorn, crack open our favorite soda, seltzer, or tea, and just talk about living more joyful lives.

Remember that joy is a spectrum of emotions, actions, and responses. Sometimes we feel joyful, sometimes we don't.

REGARDLESS OF HOW WE FEEL, WE CAN STILL CHOOSE TO ACT AND RESPOND IN JOY.

Recently I saw a sign that declared: "Introverts unite separately in your own homes."

I busted out laughing.

Whether you consider yourself an introvert or an extrovert, a quiet person or more of the party pants type, we can unite and splash joy everywhere we go.

Let's be honest: you're gonna splash something wherever you go. Why not make it joy? Don't believe me? Consider these verses from Proverbs:

> It is better to live in a corner of a roof than in a house shared with a contentious woman
> **PROVERBS 21:9, NASB**

Wow!

> A constant dripping on a day of steady rain and a contentious woman are alike.
> **PROVERBS 27:15, NASB**

Yikes! We become contentious any time we allow a disagreement or dispute to escalate to the point it causes disruption—to our workplace, our family, our children. Contention slips in when we become more concerned with winning the argument than finding a solution. Contention will drive us toward being right rather than righteous. We all fall into this at one time or another. We splash something other than joy.

> When was the last time you were, *ahem,* contentious? How did your attitude impact the lives of those you work and live with?

It happens at work a lot when I vent my frustrations in front of my workers.

✚ **BONUS ACTIVITY:**
If you put your finger in your ear and scratch, it sounds just like Pac-Man.

Rather than living like a dark storm cloud, as children of God, we're created to cheer our way through the streets heralding the arrival of God's kingdom. We're meant to pound at the door of every human heart with hilarity and celebration until the last prodigal crosses heaven's threshold, the last hardened heart is rent, and the last older brother finally plucks his fingers from his ears.

7 WAYS TO LITTER THE WORLD WITH JOY TODAY

1 **SMILE AT THE PEOPLE YOU SEE.** A recent study found that smiling can increase our happiness level and make us more productive[15], but the grin must be genuine. Start in your own home. Smile at your roommate. Your spouse. Your kids. Allow your eyes to light up, your hidden teeth to show. Look each person in the eyes. Remember that you're beaming the joy of God to them. You're reflecting the delight of your Heavenly Father.

2 **RADIATE GRACE.** When you see a coworker, spouse, or child make a mistake, do something clumsy, or break something valuable, rather than become angry, bring levity to the situation with laughter and compassion. Help them clean up the mess with a big smile and verbally affirm the person's value and worth.

3 **SING OR HUM THROUGHOUT THE DAY.** All of creation is joined as a holy chorus giving praise to God. You can join in right now, wherever you are. Turn on the radio. Plug in the iPod. Hum to yourself. Offer joyful praise to God.

4 **PLACE AN EXCLAMATION POINT ON TODAY.** Don't let this be another average day. Pause for a moment and consider what simple acts you can do to make today special for you and those you love. You don't need much time or money. Pick wildflowers or gather some fresh tree branches and place them in a vase on the table. Light a few candles. Pull out the white Christmas tree lights and hang them around your living room. Set out the fancy dishes. Wear your favorite shirt. God has placed the exclamation point of His love on your life. Do something to reflect that exclamation point, loving Him back by celebrating this day He has made.

5 **WRITE A NOTE OF BLESSING TO SOMEONE YOU LOVE.** If you need a fresh infusion of joy, then bless someone else. Grab a notecard and start jotting down all the things you appreciate about the person. Feel the gratitude well up in your heart. Then pop that notecard in the mail and spread the joy.

6 **DO SOMETHING YOU LOVE.** Most people I know aren't guilty of spending too much time doing what they love; they're guilty of doing it far too little. God has gifted and wired you for specific activities that renew your joy, fill you with delight, and remind you of His love. One of my great joys is hiking. When I experience creation, gratitude abounds in my heart, and I come home a much happier person than when I left (just ask Leif!). What is your joy-filling activity? Are you an outdoors person, a coffee shop connoisseur? Do you love shopping with friends, settling down with a great book, or cooking a new recipe? Do the activity that God uniquely wired you to thoroughly enjoy and give Him thanks for it while you're doing it. Celebrate your Creator.

7 **STRIKE UP A CONVERSATION WITH A STRANGER.** A recent study at a Chicago train station asked commuters to participate in a simple experiment. One group was asked to talk to the stranger who sat next to them. The other group was instructed to keep to themselves. By the end of the ride, the commuters who spoke to a stranger reported a more positive experience—even though most had predicted the ride would be more pleasant if they sat quiet and alone.[17] Research is beginning to reveal what I suspect God knew a long time ago—namely, that interacting with strangers helps us feel happier and more connected. Instead of keeping to yourself, say "hello" and strike up a conversation with those around you.

What would you add as another idea to litter the world with joy?

Share something you love with others - teach a craft.

Place a star ✳ by the activities you can commit to do today. Place a circle by the ones you can commit to do over the next week.

Fun, life-giving practices like these are essential to your faith. Why? The joy you radiate in the midst of your everyday life is a witness to the goodness of God. When you walk in greater amounts of joy, people are naturally drawn to you and, more importantly, to Jesus in you.

When was the last time you laughed so hard your belly ached?
Why do you think you don't laugh this hard more often?

With my boys - usually in the car or around the kitchen table. Because I don't spend more time w/ friends

Some people think that joy shines brightest on the darkest of days. But if we don't learn to radiate joy on our brightest days, then how can we beam bright when the lights go out?

This is the day to begin choosing joy, pursuing joy, and activating joy.

And, sweet friend, you don't want to miss our next gathering as we begin to discover that more than whimsy, joy is a weapon we use to fight life's battles.

♥ **CLOSING PRAYER:** Spend some time asking God to empower you to walk with greater levity and become a person who beams joy wherever you go. Ask God for opportunities to infuse laughter, humor, and hope each day.

DO THIS!! ✓✓

➕ **BONUS ACTIVITY:**

Create a joy basket. Collect items that brought you joy as a child and still place a smile on your face today— a sketch pad, bubbles, sidewalk chalk, silly putty, a booklet of word games. Tuck in some of your favorite passages on joy. The next time you're feeling blue, take some time to play and reflect on the goodness of God.

➕ **BONUS ACTIVITY:**

When you need a hearty laugh, what website, book, or movie do you turn to? Share your answers with us at *joy@margaretfeinberg.com.* We're compiling a list of suggested resources.

↑ I saw "SPY" this weekend and LOL'd

THE HIDDEN TREASURE OF JOY

GROUP GETTING STARTED: (10-15 minutes)

SESSION TWO:
THE HIDDEN TREASURE OF JOY

💬 HOMEWORK GROUP DISCUSSION

1 Share with the group three moments you recorded in your Joy Bomb Journal on page 168 in which you encountered gifts and joys from God this week.

2 In your homework from Day One, you were asked to spend time reading and reflecting on the passages of God's fierce love for you. How did this exercise affect your attitude, actions, and outlook on life this week?

3 How was your understanding or definition of joy challenged or deepened through Day Three's homework?

4 On Day Four you were asked to reflect on your favorite creational and redemptive gifts. What did you list as those you're most thankful for?

5 Share an example of something you did to litter the world with joy this past week as described on Day Five. *Smiling at people, something I love*

◀ EXPERIENTIAL ACTIVITY: COLORFUL SPLASHES OF JOY

WHAT YOU'LL NEED:
- Black markers
- Paint chips from a local hardware store in a variety of colors
- Scissors

1 Invite participants to record meaningful Scriptures about joy on several paint chips. Some may want to write a Bible verse across the whole paint sample—they make great bookmarks. Others may prefer to cut out the squares to make mini-reminders.

2 Scriptural suggestions include: Proverbs 10:28, 1 Peter 1:8-9, Romans 15:13; Isaiah 12:6; and Isaiah 35:10, in addition to each session's memory verse. Challenge participants to look up some of their own passages and share with each other.

3 Encourage participants to place these colorful squares in their car, bag, workplace, or around the house as reminders to fight back with joy.

4 Discuss the following:

Which of the Scriptures you recorded on a paint chip is most encouraging to you right now? Why?

Where do you plan to place your joy reminder?

▶ **PLAY THE SESSION TWO VIDEO: [23:40]**

Follow along with Margaret and fill in the blanks for each statement below. Take additional notes in the space provided when you hear something that resonates with you.

More than whimsy, joy is a weapon we use to __fight__ __life's__ __battles__.

Tactic 1. Joy __lifts__ __us__ __up__ when life knocks us down.

Red Balloons! UP!

Tactic 2. When our countenance falls, joy shouts __look__ __up__.

looking up - no longer focusing on the problem, but looking up to the creator

Things aren't always as they seem.

Tactic 3. Joy creates a ___holy   rackus___ that draws other near.

*how will you respond when the fight comes
up, the trials.
what if you fought back with Joy.*

Foundational Tactic:

Remain suspicious that ___God   is   up   to   something___
___good___.
What may look bad at first, could be good.

*"That's good, that's bad."
children's book.*

*we have a tendency
to compartmentalize
a shove it away.
But we should look
wider.*

Genisus 50:20

📹 VIDEO DISCUSSION

1 When you find yourself in a difficult situation, is your natural response fight, flight, or freeze? Explain.

2 In the past, which unhealthy or unhelpful weaponry have you used to face life's battles? Examples include anger, depression, spite, gossip, complaint, avoidance, addiction, etc. Which one tends to be your natural go-to choice?

3 Invite participants to take turns reading 2 Chronicles 20 out loud. Which phrases and details stand out most to you? What encourages you most from Jehoshaphat's response?

4 In what situation is it hardest for you to remain suspicious that God is up to something good right now?

5 What are three practical ways you can bring joy into that situation this week?

💜 CLOSING PRAYER

As you close in prayer ask:

- God to give each participant strength, grace, and protection for the days ahead;

- the Holy Spirit to unleash creative tactics for how to fight back with joy;

- that each participant experiences a fuller sense of God's joy in his or her life.

STARE DOWN YOUR GREATEST FEAR

THIS WEEK:

If you're following along in the trade book, read chapters ".002 The Living, Breathing Gift of Joy" and ".003 Three Simple Words to Set You Free" and dive into the five days of homework to prepare for the next gathering.

When I was a young girl, my mom would always read me a story and pray with me before tucking me in at night. She'd cast a smile over her shoulder before I'd hear the click of the light switch. That's when the darkness descended. My chest tightened. Breathing shallowed. Fear gripped me.

The slightest creak became suspect. Was that a monster moan under my bed? What caused that thump or rustle or rumble? Perhaps someone or something climbed into my closet hours before. I lay petrified of the creatures lurking in the shadows.

What did you fear most as a kid?

I remember bad dreams about alligators, being chased

As an adult, I know monsters don't reside under my bed, in the closet, or under the bathroom counter. Yet I still experience immense fear. Maybe you do, too.

NOTABLE:

Researchers are discovering that fear is a vastly personal experience. While some people become frightened watching a scary film, others are far more afraid to walk back to their cars in a dark parking lot following the film.[1]

Have you ever noticed that fears don't shrink when we ignore them? They tend to double in size. They mushroom until we're paralyzed and petrified, burrowing deeper into the darkness where there is no joy. This isn't just true when we hear a strange crackle in the bedroom as a kid. It continues as we grow older.

What are five fears that are taking up residence in your life right now?

1 *That my kids will be hurt*
2 *Not being loved*
3 *People being angry with me*
4 *Failing at work*
5 *Cats!*

Fear can serve a healthy purpose. A good dose of fear reminds us to use a seatbelt, keep our fingertips off the hot stove, and remember to lock the doors at night. Unhealthy fear can lead to worry and anxiety and subject us to a viselike control.

Consider some of the effects of living with unhealthy fear. Place a check ✓ mark by the ones you've found true in your life.

Fear causes me to:

- ☐ forget the goodness and power of God
- ☑ lose hope
- ☑ think irrationally
- ☐ become less responsive to others
- ☐ cling to safety as a god
- ☐ become risk-adverse
- ☑ love less
- ☐ feel dread
- ☑ rely more on myself
- ☐ think self-defeating thoughts rather than God-honoring ones
- ☐ experience less of life
- ☐ other: _____

📚 NOTABLE:

Didaskaleinophobia is the fear of going to school. *Ephebiphobia* is the fear of young people. *Allodoxaphobia* is the fear of opinions. *Genuphobia* is the fear of knees. *Porphyrophobia* is the fear of the color purple.

Reading through this list, I placed a check by every one. Maybe that's why Jesus is so adamant that we "fear not." Throughout the Gospels, Jesus issues more than 100 imperatives not to allow fear to get the best of us. Of these, nearly two dozen tell us to "have courage," "take heart," "do not be afraid," "do not fear," and "be of good cheer."

Jesus commands:

Take courage. I am here!
MATTHEW 14:27, NLT

Do not be afraid of those who kill the body but cannot kill the soul.
MATTHEW 10:28, NIV

So don't be afraid. You are worth much more than many sparrows.
MATTHEW 10:31, NCV

Don't be troubled or afraid.
JOHN 14:27, NLT

In this life, we will encounter situations and circumstances that cause our fears to flare. Through Christ, fear does not have to reign in our lives.

On those difficult nights as a child, I had a tough decision to make. I could burrow deeper into the blankets, strangled by fear until sleep won over, or I could confront the monsters head-on.

This required remarkable bravery for a 6-year-old. Climbing out of bed, I'd walk across the room and click on the light. With a book as a shield and a toy as a weapon, I'd tiptoe toward the closet and clutch the door handle. *Whoosh.* A few balls dropped to the floor.

I'd hunker down midway across the room to peer under the bed. Oh! A teddy bear I hadn't seen in weeks. Ever so slowly, I'd walk toward the bathroom and flip on the light. Phew. Nothing had taken up residence underneath the cabinet or behind the shower curtain. This was officially a monster-free zone.

On those scary nights, I discovered a powerful truth no matter what your age:

ONE OF THE KEYS TO OVERCOMING FEAR IS FACING FEAR.

Climbing out of the darkness and moving toward the light is hard. The unknown is far more terrifying than the known.

I want to challenge you right now to do the thing you're most afraid to do:

- Schedule the doctor's appointment.

- Go to the AA or NA or SA meeting.

- Meet with the Christian counselor.

- Break up with the guy you know you shouldn't be dating.

- Sign up for open mic night.

- See the marriage therapist.

- Schedule the colonoscopy.

- Sit down with your boss.

- Go to the dentist.

- Create a living will.

- Organize the intervention.

- Jump on the scale.

- Write the letter that's been haunting you.

- Say the thing you've been needing to say.

- Tackle that huge pile in your house or garage or storage unit.

hard conversations w/ my husband

In a cheerful shout of victory, Jesus closes His farewell discourse to the disciples: "In this world you will have trouble. But take heart! I have overcome the world" (John 16:33, NIV). "Take heart" is the Greek word *tharseo*, meaning *to have courage. Tharseo* is used six times in the Gospels, each spoken by Jesus before He performs a miracle: four times before a miraculous healing, once to settle the disciples before asking Peter to walk on water, and the final instance in John 16:33 takes place just hours before his arrest, crucifixion, and miraculous resurrection.

+ BONUS ACTIVITY:

Spend time committing Nehemiah 8:10 to memory this week. You'll find a flash card on page 193.

- Tell someone about your secret addiction.
- Schedule an appointment with the school counselor.
- Meet with an accountant to get a grip on your finances.
- Get that mole checked out.
- Call the credit card company or debt consolidator.
- Schedule the mammogram.
- Visit the grave site.
- Call the friend you haven't spoken to in years.
- Return the call you've been putting off for months.
- Have the difficult conversation with the person you love.
- Other __ask for help with weight loss or exersise__

Reflecting on this list, what is the one thing you know you need to do that you're most afraid to do?

This isn't going to be easy or fun. But sweet friend, I care about you enough to challenge you to do the hard thing.

Why? Because God can't rule your life when fear has the reins. Fear's desire is always to master us. Fear strangles us of joy, shoving us into the dark.

Today is the day of freedom. Today is the day of liberation. Today is the day you can stare down your greatest fear.

TODAY IS THE DAY TO BECOME A DOER, NOT A STEWER.

When we peek under the bed, sometimes nothing more than a collection of dust balls waits for us. The Enemy has fooled us all along. The tentacles of fear no longer have a grip on us. We are free, indeed!

Other times, the rumbling behind the closet door isn't our imagination. We stand toe-to-toe with a yellow-eyed, sharp-clawed monster.

The financial crisis is real.

The marriage is shredded.

NOTABLE:

Our bodies have an amazing physical response to fear. Fear triggers the amygdala, an almond-shaped group of nerve cells that releases a chain reaction telling your body to fight or take flight. The hypothalamus is alerted, signaling the adrenal glands to release adrenaline, glucose, and cortisol, which is why you may experience sweaty palms, an increased heart rate, and a boost of energy. When the fear is absolved, the brain returns the body to normal.[2]

Your kid is in trouble.

You need the root canal.

The friend you call isn't ready to forgive.

That pesky habit really is an addiction.

The lump is cancerous.

On the morning I found a lump in my right breast, anxiety gripped me. The last thing I wanted was to go to the doctor. Who wants to stick their womanhood in that squishy, uncomfortable pancake-maker? Who wants to find out the lump isn't benign?

I forced myself to schedule the appointment. When the technician asked if I'd noticed anything suspicious, everything in me wanted to keep quiet. Say nothing. Trust the machine to do its job.

But I spoke up.

That made all the difference. The initial test results from the mammogram were normal. It's estimated that 30 percent of all mammograms miss finding suspicious masses—which is why speaking up is so important. The only reason the doctors scheduled an ultrasound and biopsy was because I told them about the lump.

If I had remained quiet, the cancer would have continued to grow.

Staring down your greatest fear isn't easy. But we're going to do this together. I am asking you to do something critical:

Will you let someone know about this thing you need to do so he or she can pray with you and for you?

Write an email. Send a text. Pick up the phone. Visit a friend.

Staring down your greatest fear is tough stuff, and sometimes we discover that there really is a monster lurking under the bed. In those moments, you may be tempted to think living in the dark was better. Never believe that lie.

God has called you to be a child of the light (see 1 Thess. 5:5), to walk in light (see Eph. 5:8), and to bust through the darkness with the radiance of His light (see 1 John 1:7). You will never experience the fullness of joy God wants to give you when you are living in the dark.

What you find when you step out of the dark may take you by surprise, but God has known all along. He has been waiting for you to face your fear. With His help, you can overcome it.

God is whispering, "You don't face this fight alone. I am with you. I hold victory in My hands."

We will fight, sweet friend, and we will fight back with joy.

BE A WARRIOR, NOT A WORRIER.

Are you ready?

 **CLOSING PRAYER:** Spend time asking God to expose other areas of fear in your life and to show you how to stare down each one.

BONUS ACTIVITY:

Look up
1 Thessalonians 5:5,
Ephesians 5:8, and
1 John 1:7. Reflect on
what it means to be
a child of the light.

DAY TWO

PICK UP THE MOST UNLIKELY OF WEAPONS

Sometimes the divine timing in our lives is unmistakable. I spent an entire year pursuing, choosing, activating joy before I received the biopsy results.

That morning is forever ingrained in my mind.

"This is Dr. Jones," said the voice on the phone. "Is now a good time?"

It's never a good time to field a call like this, I thought.

As the physician began to speak, my head sunk into a fog. Time halted, the conversation blurred.

Carcinoma.

Positive.

Surgery.

NOTABLE:

You can read more about Margaret's journey with breast cancer in her book, *Fight Back With Joy*.

He said more, but after "carcinoma" everything grew fuzzy as if I'd been clubbed over the head. Dazed by the news, I went to find Leif.

"What's wrong?"

I never spoke a word. Leif just knew. He held me in his arms, and we stood motionless. We'd crossed a threshold from which we could never return.

In the warmth of his strong embrace, my mind wandered.

Did God ignite a desire in my heart to pursue joy in preparation for this moment? Perhaps God had been at work behind the scenes, ever so gently, getting me ready for this moment, to lay hold of a joy I'd never known before.

"We're going to fight back with joy," I said.

That was the moment I made the decision I'll never regret. I suspect that if you choose to fight back with joy you'll never regret it either. Because all of us are in a fight.

Like me, the inception might be unforgettable.

The phone call no one wants to receive.

The email you wish you could delete from your mind forever.

The photos you'd do anything to tear from your memory.

The text never meant to be sent to you.

The letter ripped open to reveal devastating news.

The image of the officer standing at your front door.

The rash words you spoke that you can never take back.

For others the inception of the fight is foggier. Perhaps you were born into combat, and you've never known a day without it. Or maybe the starting point can't be pinpointed to one moment as much as a series of mini-events. Looking in the rearview mirror, you recognize the signs and wonder how you didn't see them sooner.

Everyone's fight is different.

No one gets out of life unscathed. The fight may be against a particular disease or mental illness. Perhaps the battleground is loneliness or the desire for deeper friendships that always seem to elude you.

Maybe you find yourself contending with depression whose octopus-like tentacles keep yanking you down. Shadows of insecurity haunt you. The sense of not being enough keeps tracking you down.

The relentless tug-of-war may be for your marriage. Or kids. Or employment.

Or maybe your clash is with unhealthy thinking or eating patterns that keep looting you of vitality. Perhaps you're just struggling to hold onto that last fragment of faith.

The name and emergence of our adversities differ. You may be able to hide yours in ways that I could never hide mine. But we are all fighting.

Write down what you are fighting for in each category:

- Friends
  feeling like a bother
- Family
  did I do enough for my kids
- Relationships
- Marriage
  making Mike not love me
- Workplace
  failing - them finding out I don't know enough

- Finances
  over indulging
- Faith
  not being faithful + spending time w/God
- Physical and mental health
  weight
- Emotions
- Other:

All who find themselves in a confrontation—one they choose or one that is thrust upon them—face an important choice: What will you choose for weaponry? We can choose to fight back with the crossbow of cynicism and sling arrows of spite. Like a throwing star, we may choose sharp complaints.

SESSION TWO FIGHT BACK WITH JOY

QUOTABLE:

"Smooth seas do not make skillful sailors."
—African proverb

NOTABLE:

It's estimated that at least 1 out of 300 Americans will declare bankruptcy this year.[3] One in 8 women will be diagnosed with breast cancer,[4] and one in 7 men will be diagnosed with prostate cancer during their lives.[5] More than 40 percent of marriages in the United States end in divorce.[6] Every 67 seconds someone in the United States develops Alzheimer's.[7]

Like a whip, we may attempt to control every little detail. Or perhaps, like me, a natural lover more than fighter, you're drawn to the circular shield of denial and withdrawal.

(Circle) all the weapons you have used to fight battles in the past:

Cynicism	Sarcasm	Spite
Anger	Control	Denial
Avoidance	Withdrawal	Complaints
Busyness	Sleeplessness	Complacency
Apathy	Restlessness	Numbness
Negative thoughts	Substance abuse	Self-sufficiency
Worry	Addiction	Despair

Over the years, I watched other people use these weapons, and I even tried many on for size myself. But I discovered the hard way that despite their accessibility and ease of use, they don't win battles.

From the first day of diagnosis, I knew I needed a different kind of weapon for this formidable foe. After many months of studying joy, I knew I'd only scratched the surface of this powerful armament. I realized my pursuit of joy wasn't an accident. It was preparation for what was coming.

FORCED ONTO THE BATTLEGROUND TO FACE AN UNKNOWN AND OMINOUS FOE, I DECIDED TO FIGHT BACK WITH JOY.

Joy is an unusual choice for weaponry, but throughout the Bible we find God sending people into battle with the most unlikely and strange ammunition.

Look up each of the passages to fill in the chart below.

Bible Passage	Weaponry	Outcome
Exodus 17:8-13	sword	Amalekite army
Exodus 23:28-30	hornets	Possession of the land
Joshua 6:2-20	trumplets	took the city
Judges 15:14-16	Spirit of the lord	free from bondage
1 Samuel 17:40-50	slingshot + stone	defeat the Philistine

One of the most powerful and popular examples of God's people girding themselves with joy is found in the book of Nehemiah. This Old Testament leader was sent to rebuild the city of Jerusalem after being destroyed by the Babylonian army more than a century before.

Rather than give into the despairing situation, Nehemiah chooses to fight back with joy. He shifts his focus. He begins to familiarize himself with stone and mortar while his buddy, Ezra, works through Scripture. Side-by-side, they team up to restore the walls of the once-great metropolis and the holiness of God's people.

What oppositions did Nehemiah face during the construction according to Nehemiah 6:1-9?

Sanballat attempt to distract them from the work.

Despite a variety of challenges, Nehemiah finishes the project in record time—52 days. The reconstruction of the wall serves as a physical representation of the spiritual need of rebuilding among God's people. Upon completion, the people gather as Ezra recites the teachings of Moses. The crowds weep for their shortcomings as they hear God's law proclaimed.

Then, Nehemiah does something startling—he instructs the people to dry their eyes and celebrate:

> Do not grieve, for the joy of the LORD is your strength.
> **NEHEMIAH 8:10, NIV**

 NOTABLE:

The Babylonian Exile was a 70-year period in Jewish history where many Jews were forced into Babylon after Nebuchadnezzar, king of the Chaldeans, conquered Jerusalem, destroying the temple. When Persia's Cyrus the Great captured Babylon, he released the Jews back to Jerusalem to rebuild. Jews that remained in Babylon were part of the diaspora.

NOTABLE:

Ezra, whose name means "help," worked hand-in-hand with Nehemiah to restore the landscape and the hearts of God's people.

Nehemiah instructs the people to throw a party. Light the grill. Hang the streamers. Slather the cake with extra icing. Send to-go portions to those who have nothing—the strangers and servants, the orphans and widows—even the poor should partake in the fiesta.

Nehemiah knows that when we feel weak, merrymaking makes us mighty. We cannot continue in any endeavor for very long apart from joy. Without gladness, even the best spiritual practices lose their vitality and staying power.

MORE THAN WHIMSY, JOY IS A WEAPON WE USE TO FIGHT LIFE'S BATTLES.

That's why joy is so crucial. When it comes to the fights of life, we need joy to be our companion. Joy does three crucial things:

1 JOY ELEVATES US WHEN WE FACE OVERWHELMING CIRCUMSTANCES.

Like a helium-filled red balloon, joy gives us levity in life. Maybe you had a morning like I did yesterday. The alarm went off. I tugged the covers over my head. My limbs hung heavy. That day's doctor appointment seemed more than I could bear. Rather than give into the weighty discouragement, I decided to activate joy in the midst of my circumstances and offer thanks to God. I thanked Him that I live in a country with access to some of the world's best medical care. I thanked God for the compassionate medical team He provided. I thanked Him for the day that He had made. Somehow in giving thanks, I found my joy renewed.

Life felt a little lighter. And I did, too.

Joy provided the lift I needed to face the day. When we're tempted to declare, "I can't!," joy strengthens our resolve. "God, You can!"

On the continuum below, mark how much levity you're experiencing in the situation you're facing.

●————————————————●————————————————●

I have no levity in
the situation I'm facing.

I am able to experience levity
in the situation I'm facing.

2 JOY REFOCUSES OUR ATTENTION ON GOD.

Not only does joy infuse our stride in life, but it also changes our perspective. Imagine yourself holding a handful of those helium-filled

---

NOTABLE:

Nehemiah, whose name means "comforted by God," ushers that same consolation to God's people when he says, "Do not grieve, for the joy of the Lord is your strength."

red balloons. Feel the tug of the red ribbons against your palm and fingers. Notice the way each inflated bulb floats ever so gently. Now, consider your posture.

Just as clinging to the balloons invites us to raise our eyes in admiration, so, too, does joy. Its presence is an invitation to do one of the simplest yet most powerful things a follower of Jesus can do: look up! Refocus our attention on God. Seek Him as the source of all satisfaction and pleasure.

No matter what adversity we face, we can choose to refocus from what's before us, toward the God who fills us with joy. Instead of seeing the adversity, we become alert to Christ who has overcome all things and for whom nothing is impossible.

What situation are you facing right now that has distracted your focus from God?

Being consumed with work + daily life.

3 **JOY DRAWS OTHERS TO CHRIST.**

Joy is a powerful magnet for sharing the gospel. When you walk into a dark, formidable situation with joy, people turn their heads. Happiness and levity are the last things they expect to see.

Time and time again, I found that whenever I walked in joy—even through difficult medical appointments and treatments, people noticed. One nurse even stopped me to ask, "Where do you get this kind of joy?"

How does the love, joy, and hope inside us transform the world around us according to Matthew 5:13-16?

our light can give light to those around us.

When was the last time you noticed your joyful disposition drawing others to Christ?

ummm ... it's been a while

What other advantages do you see to fighting with joy?

It's hard to feel sorrow or sorry for yourself when you are focusing on Joy.

Fighting back with joy is a powerful spiritual discipline. Here are some of the truths I'm discovering along the way. Underline the statements that ring true to you.

- When we fight back with joy, we declare that the <u>darkness does not win.</u>

- When we fight back with joy, we embrace the deepest reality of our identity, which is <u>not weary and beaten down,</u> but beloved and joyful.

- When we fight back with joy, we are confident that God is with us and for us.

- When we fight back with joy, we do so with the assurance that we're held in the <u>tender arms</u> of the One greater than us.

- When we fight back with joy, we set our eyes on an eternal reality that is more tangible than what we're enduring.

- When we fight back with joy, we are deeply convinced that the battle has already been won through Christ.

Now let me ask you: What does it mean for you to fight back with joy in the midst of your circumstances?

finding the bright side. Not being overcome by the darkness

As we close this lesson, can I pray for you?

Dear Jesus, I don't know what battlefield my sweet friend is on right now—whether the fight involves family, marriage, finances, health, or something only the two of you know about. I pray, right now, that You would fill my friend with exceeding joy. I pray that joy would swell in my friend's heart, giving strength, courage, and hope. And I ask that the joy of Your presence would sustain my friend in the days ahead. Father, we know victory rests with You. And we entrust ourselves wholly and fully to You. In Jesus' name. Amen.

KNOCK DOWN THE JOY BLOCKERS

Up to this point, we examined the abundant joy of God. We explored how joy commences in God. Postcards of God's generosity and joy are seen in creational and redemptive gifts. We also looked at joy as weaponry, a source of strength for the battles of life.

Before we can step on the battlefield ready to fight back with joy, we need to ensure nothing is blocking, stealing, or draining our joy.

I confess, some days joy feels a million miles away. My joy-o-meter lingers at zero. Fighting back with joy is impossible when your joy tank is bone-dry.

On those days, I use tactics I've already shared with you. I'll spend time reading passages that declare God's fierce love for me. I'll count my joys and give thanks to God for His goodness and generosity. When the house is empty, I'll offer some rowdy expressions of praise. If I remain joyless, it's time for deeper self-reflection.

Just as the Bible reveals God as joyful and the Joy-Giver, it also highlights that in which God does not take pleasure or delight.

QUOTABLE:

"We must fight against our very natures to become the joy-filled people of God. We must fight our sin and countless distractions."
—Angela Thomas, author, speaker, and my sweet friend[9]

Fill out the chart below with those things in which God takes no delight.

SCRIPTURE	GOD'S LACK OF DELIGHT
Psalm 5:4	he does not delight in evil
Isaiah 9:16-17	people who mislead others + guide them astray
Isaiah 65:12	those who don't listen + do evil.
Ezekiel 35:14-15	those who rejoice at others loss
Proverbs 6:16-19	haughty eyes, lying tongue, wicked heart, false witness....

In some circumstances, God will even take away joy.

King David experiences this loss of joy after committing adultery with Bathsheba and ordering the murder of her husband. David doesn't think twice about his actions. Though we read the story with a bit of shock, the actions David takes seem justifiable to him. They are within his power and rule.

David doesn't recognize his wrongdoing until someone else exposes it. When the prophet Nathan uncovers the king's sin, David's response is one of remorse and repentance.

Psalm 51:11-12 (NIV), written after the king's behavior is made public, says:

> Do not cast me from your presence or take your Holy
> Spirit from me. Restore to me the joy of your salvation
> and grant me a willing spirit, to sustain me.

David asks not to be exiled from the presence of God, the source of all joy. He requests that the joy of His salvation—the origin of the redemptive gifts of God—be renewed in His life.

David's story reminds us that sin and disobedience are among the great joy blockers in our lives. Few things will barricade joy like disregarding God and His commands. And we can't fight back with joy if we don't have joy.

A few weeks ago, I felt joyless. The world felt grainy, life seemed colorless. We all have bad days, but one snowballed into the next and next. Prayer felt empty. Even the most joyful words of the Bible read flat and disconnected. My countenance was marked by more of a scowl than a smile. My fuse ran short with everyone in almost every situation. Everyday inconveniences were magnified 10 times.

I was annoyed with everything—including myself. I didn't even want to be around myself. Do you ever have those days?

Describe the last time you had a joyless day—a day when everything annoyed, irritated, and frustrated you.

This happens at work, one thing goes wrong and everything else is colored by that event.

Reaching a point of desperation, I cried out to God. Something was separating me from the joy of the Lord. I found my answer tucked in Psalm 32. The psalmist paints a portrait of someone who felt like I did.

NOTABLE:
To better understand the difference between God taking pleasure in His people and taking pleasure in causing ruin, read Deuteronomy 28. God is so committed to our holiness that He will even allow destruction if it draws us back to Him.

According to Psalm 32, what caused David to lose joy? What is the physical response to his loss of joy?

Confess to the Lord the things that you are guilty of.

How is his joy restored?

Sins are forgiven and God becomes our refuge.

Describe a situation where you experienced a similar countenance change—from joyless to joyful. What made the difference?

Getting out what is bothering me; either confessing or just having a discussion. And of course realizing things aren't so bad.

This psalm reminded me that I needed to pause for a time of self-examination:

- Lord, where have I allowed sin into my life?
- Have I done anything against You that's blocking me from receiving the gift of Your joy?
- Have I done anything against You that's caused my joy to be taken away?
- Am I holding on to any anger, unforgiveness, or bitterness toward others?
- What can I do to bring healing and reconciliation?

As I reflected on these questions, I remembered something that happened the week before. A stranger gave us a check to help with the mountain of medical bills we were facing. The gift was not only much needed, but a powerful reminder of God's provision in our lives. And the person who gave us the check didn't realize that the gift could not be more aptly timed. It arrived on the day before my birthday.

My husband, Leif, lost the check. We searched the washer and dryer, our suitcases, every countertop, even dug through our dog Hershey's toys. The gift was gone—along with it the name of the person who had given the gift. We couldn't even say thank you.

At the time, I told Leif that it was "no big deal." But it was a very big deal, something significant to me.

Anger festered in my heart until roots sprouted and spread, infecting my

NOTABLE:

The story of David and Bathsheba plays out like a bad soap opera. Not only was Bathsheba the wife of one of King David's honored soldiers (Uriah—2 Sam. 23:39), she was also the granddaughter of one of his most trusted advisors (Ahithophel— 2 Sam. 16:23), and the daughter of one of his best warriors (Eliam—2 Sam. 23:34).

QUOTABLE:

"Search me, God, and know my heart; test me and know my anxious thoughts. See if there is any offensive way in me, and lead me in the way everlasting."
—Psalm 139:23-24, NIV

attitude, my countenance, my demeanor. Some of the frustration was directed toward myself. Why did I trust Leif to keep track of the check? I should have done that myself. Every financial strain became a reminder. Crabbiness soon spread to the insurance company, the bills that flooded in, the clients who refused to pay. Anger's fruit blossomed in my life until I could almost taste the bitterness and resentment. Before I knew what happened, every last droplet of joy evaporated from my life.

On the first meter below, fill in how much unforgiveness, bitterness, or anger you harbor. On the second meter, fill in where your joy-o-meter rests. Do you see any relationship between the two? Explain.

EMPTY			X			FULL

Unforgiveness, Bitterness, Anger

EMPTY		X				FULL

Joy-O-Meter

NOTABLE:

Scientists are beginning to study the health benefits of forgiveness. These include lower blood pressure and heart rate, improved sleep, decreased physical complaints of aches and pain, lower stress, reduced depression, improved relationships, and increased optimism.

If I wanted to experience the joy of being a child of God again, I needed forgiveness. I asked God to forgive me for harboring anger and unforgiveness. Then, I knew I needed to forgive my husband.

Leif and I initiated a practice early in our marriage that we continue more than a decade later. Whenever one of us becomes angry or upset with the other person, we must do three things:

1 **TELL THE OTHER PERSON WHAT MADE US UPSET.**

2 **TELL THE OTHER PERSON THAT WE FORGIVE HIM OR HER.**

3 **SAY THREE SWEET THINGS WE LIKE ABOUT THE OTHER PERSON.**

BONUS ACTIVITY:

The next time your coworker, spouse, or friend does something upsetting, follow these three steps. Tell him or her what upset you, extend forgiveness, and say three kind things about that person. Notice how this practice affects your attitude and relationship.

This helps us become better communicators, avoid future unnecessary disputes, and engage in the process of forgiving and blessing one another.

After confessing to Leif that the lost check was a big deal to me, I chose to forgive him. Then, I offered three compliments: I'm so grateful to be married to you. I couldn't be more proud of the kindness you show others. I love getting to live life with you.

Something about the process of forgiveness unlatched the floodgate of joy in my heart. I felt lighter. Forgiving myself and extending grace to others felt easier. My countenance changed. Bounce returned to my step.

When I seek God and ask Him where I need to repent, I'm awed by how soon a particular situation or circumstance comes to mind. A person who wronged me, and I never forgave. An interaction where I felt shortchanged. Though I say "no big deal" with my lips, it festers in my heart. Or a judgment I'd made about someone else that was harsh and unfair. The weight of the flippant comment followed me. These sins became joy blockers.

When I stop to ask God to reveal my sin, I'm awestruck by the way He answers. As I take time to ask forgiveness and bless those who have caused pain or harm, my joy tank refills. I feel lighter and more thankful.

What is the connection between joy and forgiveness in Psalm 86:4-5?

God brings us both, joy + forgiveness.

Take a few moments right now to do a little self-examination. Ask the Holy Spirit:

- Where have I allowed sin into my life?
- Have I done anything against You that's blocking me from receiving the gift of Your joy?
- Have I done anything against You that's caused my joy to be taken away?
- Am I holding on to any anger, unforgiveness, or bitterness toward others?
- What can I do to bring healing and reconciliation?

Write down the people, circumstances, and situations that come to mind. Then one by one, ask God's forgiveness for each. Ask God if there's anything you need to do for restitution or healing in the situation. Consider ways you can bless those who have harmed you.

My conversations at work about my dissatisfaction with my non-promotion. Lack of professionalism. With God I've been distant. Leaving my study to last minute too. Resentment about finances with Mike + I.

QUOTABLE:

"If we confess our sins, he is faithful and just and will forgive us our sins and purify us from all unrighteousness."
—1 John 1:9, NIV

QUOTABLE:

"Just so, I tell you, there is joy before the angels of God over one sinner who repents."
—Luke 15:10, ESV

My hope and prayer is that as you walk in greater forgiveness, you will experience more joy and levity in your life. May the sense of blessedness and being wholly and completely forgiven fill you with delight.

💚 **CLOSING PRAYER:** Thank God for the forgiveness He offers through Jesus. Thank Him for His faithfulness to forgive our sins and remove the joy blockers in our lives.

PUSH BACK JOY ROBBERS

Earlier today, I hopped online to catch up with some friends on Facebook and Instagram. I adore looking at people's photos and hearing their latest news. But for some reason today I wasn't as excited and found myself face-to-face with a joy robber.

Carrie updated that she and Mark purchased a brand new car with every bell and whistle you can imagine. The kind of car we could never afford. Melodee shared that her family is going to Disney World next month. We could really use a vacation. Brenda just got a promotion that came with stock options. I wonder what that feels like. Jim and Cindy tagged all the kids and grandkids in their matching, smiling family portrait. Must be nice to have your extended family all living in the same town. Becky checked in at the gym, again. Who has that kind of energy? Sarah snapped a picture of her latest Pinterest-worthy craft. Who has that kind of time? Len just scored concert tickets to hear one of my favorite bands. Why didn't I try to win? And Emily and James still look like the cutest, cuddliest newlyweds after eight years of marriage. How do they do it?

Social media whispered, "All your friends have better lives." Everyone's kids are adorable, happy, and well behaved. Their careers appear far more successful. Their dogs pose on command. Their houses display smart designs. Their hobbies look extra interesting. The images portrayed colorful, beautiful, accomplished lives.

Swoop. I'd fallen into the comparison trap again. Tumbling to the bottom, I could hear my balloons of joy *pop, pop,* popping.

✚ **BONUS ACTIVITY:**

Don't forget to continue adding moments when you've experienced joy from God to your Joy Bomb Journal.

💬 **QUOTABLE:**

"The distorted lens of social media amplifies the temptation to draw comparisons. When practicing Christian women compare themselves to their friends through social media such as Facebook, Twitter, or Pinterest, they are 11 times more likely to say their friends have more status and privilege and 10 times more likely to say others are more creative. They are also more likely to believe others have a better career and a superior ability to accomplish tasks." — Barna Group Research[10]

...paring ourselves to others never leads to true joy, but rather can lead to a ...sense of joy known as *schadenfreude*. This German word can be translated ...*age-joy* and describes a kind of malicious joy in the misfortune of others. ...s shrill cry from true joy.

...hen was the last time you slipped into practicing schadenfreude?

Everyday. I compare others work, their size clothes, hair, organization skills, success. REALLY BAD HABIT. — *Faith*

What does Proverbs 24:17-18 reveal about this response?

Do not be envious or take pleasure in others failures.

📚 NOTABLE:

Three ways to fight back against the comparison trap:

1. Thank God that He made you unique with particular skills and talents.

2. Build the other person up by looking for every opportunity to celebrate his or her God-given gifts and blessings.

3. Be grateful for the diversity found among God's creation. Everyone is uniquely gifted to introduce others to Christ and bring God glory.

Not only do we need to be aware of the hidden sins of our hearts, we also need to live on high alert for the everyday joy robbers that can so easily slink into our lives. These are sneaky little buggers. They don't tend to cart away all the joy God has given us in a single swoop; they pilfer a little at a time. If joy is represented by a huge fistful of balloons, then these joy thieves come and clip one strand one day, pop a balloon another day, tug one out of our fingers when we're not looking a few days later. Suddenly we look up and all our joy is gone.

I wish the comparison trap was the only joy robber in my life, but it's one of many.

Maybe you recognize a few of these joy robbers in your life. As you read through the following, circle the robbers who are common visitors in your life right now:

~~Fear~~	Regret	Shame	~~Guilt~~
Anxiety	Worry	Anger	Perfectionism
~~Comparison~~	Resentment	~~Frustration~~	~~Depression~~
Despair	Busyness	Exhaustion	Weariness
~~Discontentment~~	Denial	Other:	

My hunch is that the joy robbers you've circled aren't new to you. They have been around for a while—possibly many years. No matter how long they've taken up residence in your life, God desires to set you free. He longs for you to live a life liberated from these joy robbers, a life in which you experience the fullness of joy He has for you.

Will you take time right now to talk to Jesus about each joy robber you circled?

1. Ask Jesus what the root or backstory of the joy robber is in your life. Where did it come from? Was there a particular incident in the past, possibly your childhood, through which this joy robber moved in?

2. Ask Jesus to reveal what lies the joy robber has been whispering in your ear. Sometimes joy robbers say nasty, untrue things like, "You're not loved," "You'll never measure up," "You'll never be enough," "You have to do it all on your own," and, "It's all your fault."

3. Ask Jesus to reveal the truth of what He thinks of you. Consider using the Bible to look up meaningful passages or reflect on Scripture from pages 16-17 that reveals how fiercely God loves you.

4. Ask Jesus to remove this joy robber from your life once and for all through the power of His death and resurrection on the cross (see John 8:36). Ask the Holy Spirit to reveal to you whenever the joy robber may try to break in over the next few days and to give you strength to resist.

5. Thank God for His love, protection, and the joy He continues to give you.

As I walked through each of these steps with one of my biggest joy robbers, the comparison trap, I found my balloons of joy slowly being refilled. Instead of scrolling through posts on social media and seething with envy, I celebrated with my friends and loved ones. Instead of comparing my marriage, my home, and my job with everyone else's, I was expressing gratitude for the good gifts God has given me. Instead of weighing myself on the world's scale, I allowed the truth of my identity in God to saturate and sustain me. I could already feel the burden lifting, joy being restored.

Kicking these joy robbers to the curb won't be a one-and-done tactic. Bookmark or dog-ear these pages as a resource to return to whenever you sight a new joy robber trying to break into your life.

If we're going to fight back with joy, then we have to fortify our lives for those things that steal our joy. One big joy thief remains that we need to conquer in the final day's homework this week: a lack of rest.

CLOSING PRAYER: Spend time asking God to continue revealing any joy robbers in your life and resist them through prayer, the truth of Scripture, and the encouraging stories of others who have overcome.

+ BONUS ACTIVITY:

I'd love to hear your wisdom on removing the joy robbers from life. Email me at *joy@ margaretfeinberg.com.*

QUOTABLE:

"We fail to open our hands to be filled with God's bounty because our hands are clasped on other things, or we have confused pleasing God with appeasing God. But when we engage in our relationship with God with joy and dancing, in play, no matter what our age, we 'please God' by taking pleasure in the gift of life and relationship with the Creator and spreading that joy to others. In God's pleasure, we are blessed, and thus can be a blessing to others." — Leonard Sweet, author[11]

BANISH THE JOY SWINDLER

Last night was a tough night. I tossed and turned so many times I knocked our superpup, Hershey, off the bed. I woke up at 11:30 p.m., 1:00 a.m., 2:14 a.m., and then laid in the darkness until nearly 4:45 a.m., when Leif's alarm went off.

This morning I am groggy, edgy, murky. I snapped at Leif for his early alarm, complained about the chilly weather, and griped about the full trash can—all before my first cup of coffee. It's amazing the heavy toll a lack of sleep can take on our lives.

A few years ago someone asked me, "What's the biggest trigger for sin in your life?" My answer: "Lack of sleep!"

When I get a good night's rest, I'm more patient and kind. I don't tend to overeat or become bothered by nuisances. Without rest, every difficulty and hardship magnifies. My eyes skip like rocks from one problem to the next.

One of the biggest joy swindlers in our lives is a lack of rest.

How does loss of sleep affect your attitude and actions?

I get headaches and therefore am impatient + less joyful. Think Sunday at Crops

As I've been diving into Scripture, one of the things I've been discovering is that joy and rest are intimately linked. The equation looks something like this:

$$\boxtimes REST = \boxtimes JOY$$

Increased rest leads to increased joy. As we learn to find our rest in God and make time to rest, our joy naturally expands. Consider Isaiah 58:13–14 (NIV):

> If you call the Sabbath a delight and the LORD's holy
> day honorable, and if you honor it by not going your
> own way and not doing as you please or speaking idle
> words, then you will find your joy in the LORD, and I will
> cause you to ride in triumph on the heights of the land
> and to feast on the inheritance of your father Jacob.

NOTABLE:

Large-scale studies reveal that a lack of sleep leads to weight gain over time. A single night of sleep deprivation makes fattening, high-calorie foods more attractive and at the same time interferes with the brain's ability to override desire with rational decision-making.[12]

What five things does God ask us to do according to this passage?

1 not go your own way

2 not doing as you please

3 speaking idle words

4 call the Sabbath a delight

5 call his day honorable

What is the reward of obedience?

you will find your joy in the lord, Ride in triumph, feast on the inheritance

Isaiah uses rich imagery in this passage. The idea of taking a "ride in triumph on the heights of the land" makes me want to squeal in glee. Sitting down to a feast that's centered on God's faithfulness, well, count me in. The prophet gives us a vibrant portrait of the joy that comes when we enter the rest God has for us.

Most of us find ourselves in seasons of living in overdrive. Holidays, pressing work deadlines, and the kick-off of the school year are among many seasons when we can find ourselves doing too much and giving into our performance-driven culture. But if we go for too long without rest and rejuvenation, we could be on our way to burn out.

Take the Burn Out Quiz to find out if you are on your way to burn out. Circle the response that best describes you.

Your first response to waking up in the morning is to:

A. Jump out of bed and start cooking breakfast for everyone;

B. Feel groggy and stumble your way to the coffee maker;

C. Lay in bed second guessing if you can make it through the day;

D. Pull the covers over your head and turn off the alarm clock—today is too much.

You turn to caffeine or sugar for boosts:

A. Once a month

B. A few days a week

C. Every day

D. Every hour

At work or as a stay-at-home parent, you:

    A. Couldn't be happier;

    B. Are far from perfect, but you enjoy your work;

    C. Are barely keeping up;

    D. Are past due for a change in career or daily schedule.

If you answered mostly A's, you are operating in your sweet spot. You've found a beautiful balance between everyday tasks and taking time to care for yourself. Spend some time thanking God for being a source of rest and restoration for you.

If you answered mostly B's, you are in a healthy place. As long as you keep developing healthy boundaries and don't overextend yourself, you'll be able to steer clear of burnout and be a blessing and encouragement to many.

If you answered mostly C's, you're well on your way to burnout. The good news is you're not there yet. If you aggressively begin making changes in your commitment levels and schedule, you're going to discover more time to rest and reconnect with God.

If you answered mostly D's, it may be time for a schedule makeover. The burnout is taking a heavier toll than you realize on your body, mind, spirit, and emotions. Talk to a spouse or friend, and let that person know what's going on. Ask him or her to join you in praying for healthy solutions to get you on a more vibrant, joy-filled track of life.

Through answering God's call to rest, we are filled with more joy. Apart from rest, our joy is swindled away—as is our resilience.

My counselor said something startling to me last week:

"Margaret, you know that your resilience is finite."

"Excuse me?" I pressed. "Every time I push hard and then rest, I find myself bouncing back."

"That can only last for so long, so many years," the counselor said. "If you don't take care of your body, mind, and emotions through proper rest, you'll find that one day you can burn a hole through your resilience. Bouncing back becomes harder until it doesn't happen at all."

The counselor's words stunned me. I knew deep inside he was right.

NOTABLE:

Over 70 percent of Americans leave vacation days unused. The average American will leave or roll over 12 vacation days each year.[15]

Circle the answer you've found most true. Explain. Resilience is:

FINITE   INFINITE

I thought it was infinite because I keep being able to keep up the pace.

Describe a time you came close to burning a hole in your resilience.

So much on my plate that I couldn't take anymore and I became less + less effective + more short tempered.

📖 **NOTABLE:**

Honoring the Sabbath is the fourth and longest of the Ten Commandments. The Hebrew word for Sabbath is *sabbat*, meaning *stopping* or *ceasing*. Ceasing our work is an act of trusting that God holds everything together, not us.

That's one reason God gives us the Sabbath. This day is meant to be more than just 24 hours off work. It is a time set apart for us to enjoy God, His creation (including each other), and the fruits of our labor. This is a day for our joy tanks to be refueled. This is a time and space set apart for every fiber of our being to experience renewal and regeneration.

Remember that God celebrated the first Sabbath after declaring that which He made as "very good" (see Gen. 1:31). He took time to enjoy all that He had made. If God took time to enjoy the Sabbath, how much more should you and I?

What are three things that prevent you from practicing the Sabbath?

1 *It's a day I can finally get stuff done*
2 *Guilt of not doing anything*
3 *Sometimes the less I do, the more worn I feel*

For me, the Sabbath used to be a holy rule. Take a day off. Check. Over the last few years I've been discovering the invitation to partake in Sabbath is a gift and life-changing spiritual practice. Sleep in. Take a catnap. Fall asleep while reading a good book.

As I withdraw from work, my eyes and heart begin to open to new joys all around. My pace slows. Food tastes more sweet and flavorful. Details long overlooked in the busyness of life are appreciated. Nature's beauty appears more vibrant. Sabbath helps me see and savor the "little joys" all around.

Rewrite Mark 2:27 in your own words.

The sabbath was made for man, not man for the Sabbath.
It is a gift given to me to rest.

When was the last time you celebrated the Sabbath and took a day off to rest and reconnect with God? How did the practice help you discover any "little joys"?

I think I take partial days. But I feel guilt instead of joy.

Now, I know that for some of you who are single parents, juggling multiple jobs, or trying to get something on the table for the kids besides chicken nuggets, the idea of taking an entire day off might be a stretch. But Jesus is still inviting you to enter into His rest.

Circle the words that describe you right now:

Worried	Overloaded	Maxed out	Worn
Striving	Spread thin	Exhausted	Busy
On edge	Stressed	In a tizzy	Anxious
Wake up tired	Go to bed late	Overwhelmed	Too little time

If you circled one or more of these, I'm glad you're here! I know there are to-do lists vying for your time. You're the exact person Jesus is speaking to when He says:

Come to me, all you who are weary and burdened, and I will give you rest. Take my yoke upon you and learn from me, for I am gentle and humble in heart, and you will find rest for your souls. For my yoke is easy and my burden is light.

MATTHEW 11:28-30, NIV

This is an invitation that Jesus extends to us every day, all day. We can begin looking for windows of time when we answer, "Yes! Jesus, give me your rest!"

> **QUOTABLE:**
>
> "For thus said the Lord GOD, the Holy One of Israel, 'In returning and rest you shall be saved; in quietness and in trust shall be your strength.' But you were unwilling."
> —Isaiah 30:15, ESV

> **QUOTABLE:**
>
> "A sense of rest ... is where the good creation of Genesis 1 originally concluded on the seventh day, before its disruption in the chapters that follow. What we find otherwise is a sense of restlessness. Thus, if there is anything that summarizes the Pentateuch's vision of the good and happy life it is rest. Rest at the end of a life well lived, rest together at the communal meal at the end of the harvest, rest in the Promised Land." —Nathan MacDonald, professor[16]

I'm shy about sharing it with you, but I have a secret daily practice I started a few months ago that I haven't told anyone about. It's my way of learning to pause and catch my breath in the midst of every day.

Fresh berries are among my most favorite foods on the planet. Raspberries. Strawberries. Blueberries. Blackberries.

I'll buy whatever berries are in season and on sale. In the middle of the afternoon, I rinse a handful in a white bowl. I saunter to a window to admire the puffy clouds and oceanic sky. Perhaps a bunny will be sunbathing in our yard or a bird perched on an Aspen tree branch.

Eyeing the natural wonders, I relish the berries. One by one. Experiencing the sweetness, the flavor, the texture. I admire the beauty of God all around. As I see and savor and enter into God's rest, I quote the following verse:

> Taste and see that the LORD is good;
> blessed is the one who takes refuge in him.
> PSALM 34:8, NIV

I'm embarrassed by my silly, little spiritual practice. Yet every time I do it, I feel more rested, and, well, more joyful.

Here are three ways I am going to carve out moments of rest this week:

- Steal away time each afternoon to savor my raspberries.
- Hop in bed 30 minutes earlier tonight.
- Slip in a walk around the neighborhood between errands.

What are three ways *you* are going to carve out moments of rest this week?

- *Take a lunch hour - 30 minutes no work*
- *Start my puzzle or color a little*
-

One of my friends developed a practice that makes me chuckle. Paula has a minivan full of kids under the age of 5. We cheer on the days she can find a few minutes to take a shower, let alone brush her teeth. No matter how crazy, pull-her-hair-out busy her days become, she always sneaks in a few minutes when the kids are napping to do something that breathes life into her soul.

Paula pulls a huge tub of cookie dough from the freezer and bakes herself four chocolate chunk cookies. On good days, she says, the cookies are small. On the rougher days, those cookies fill the pan. The number of cookies never changes. Just the size. Then she nestles on her couch, eats the cookies, and thanks God for her blessed family.

Paula has done this for so long that if you visit her home you'll spy a singed stain on the couch from the corner of the hot cookie pan.

If only we all had the metabolism to eat four cookies every day.

My hunch is that each of us can be intentional about entering into the rest God has for us, experiencing more joy, and tasting and seeing the goodness of God all around.

✚ BONUS ACTIVITY:

Look up Psalm 46:10. The NASB reads, "Cease striving." How are you striving right now? How does knowing God allow you to be still and cease striving?

What meaningful practice will remind you to taste and see the Lord's goodness and breathe in rest?

Make my coffee at home + take 5-10 minutes on the deck to enjoy it.

The next video teaching is just around the corner, and it's one you're not going to want to miss! Now that we've established joy as our weapon and banished the joy thieves, we're going to learn tactics for how to fight back with joy every day.

♥ CLOSING PRAYER: Ask God to help you set aside time on a regular basis to celebrate the Sabbath and enter into the rest that Christ wants to give you each day.

POKE HOLES IN THE DARKNESS

GROUP GETTING STARTED: (10-15 minutes)

SESSION THREE:
POKE HOLES IN THE DARKNESS

HOMEWORK GROUP DISCUSSION

1. Share with the group three moments you recorded in your Joy Bomb Journal on page 168 in which you encountered gifts and joys from God this week.

2. In the homework from Day One, you were asked about the one thing you know you need to do but fear most. Did you do it? Why or why not? What was the outcome?

3. On Day Two you explored what you are fighting for. How can the people in your study group support you in your fight?

4. On Day Four you were challenged to reflect on joy robbers in your life. What is one joy robber you kicked to the curb through the time of prayer?

5. When do you plan to set apart a day of rest as described in Day Five?

EXPERIENTIAL ACTIVITY: A JOY HUNT

WHAT YOU'LL NEED:
- One balloon per person
- Colorful permanent markers (at least one per person)

1. Pass out one balloon and marker per person. Ask participants to blow up their balloon. Consider bringing a balloon pump for those who are unable or blow some up ahead of time.

2. Using a marker, ask participants to write their answers to the following five fill-in-the-blank statements on their balloons.

When I'm joyful, people can tell by my _____.

My most joyful memory from this year was _____.

I feel great joy when I think about _____.

Surprisingly, I feel joy when I _____.

One idea of something joyful we could do as a group is _____.

3 Take time for everyone to share their answers. Then, have everyone throw their balloons on the floor in the center of the group.

4 When everyone has shared and tossed their balloons in the center, discuss the following:

- *How do the balloons represent how much we have to celebrate in our lives?*
- *In what ways is sharing our responses with one another a means of fighting back with joy?*
- *How did this activity bring a sense of "party" to everyday living?*

▶ **PLAY THE SESSION THREE VIDEO: [25:15]**

Follow along with Margaret and fill in the blanks for each statement below. Take additional notes in the space provided when you hear something that resonates with you.

Tactic 1. March forth with __mirth__.

LAUGH BOX!

mirth - a joyful out break of laughter

laughter is the only language that everyone understands.

Proverbs: cheerful heart
Psalms 104:26
*Sachaq - laugh amuse, be joyful OR joke

Poke holes in the darkness until it bleeds light.

Tactic 2. Embrace celebration as a ___discipline___.

Sometimes you have to will yourself to celebrate.

Neiamiah: 8:9-12   Do not grieve for the joy of the Lord is your strength.

Toss confetti when you least feel like it.

Tactic 3. Recognize that your Heavenly Father wants to ___speak   to   you___.

God whispers to us in our pleasures, but he shouts in our pain. - C.S. Lewis

Hebrews 11 - walk of fame.

words sounding trite + cliche

Isaiah 36:4
Cabal - carry the load.

VIDEO DISCUSSION

1 Who serves as a laugh box in your life, helping you to walk lighter?
2 What are some of your favorite go-to sources of comedy and laughter?
3 In what area of your life do you need to practice celebration as a discipline?
4 Invite a participant to read John 16:13 aloud. Have you ever experienced God speaking to you in the wake of difficult circumstances? What did you sense the Holy Spirit saying? How did those words affect you?

CLOSING PRAYER

As you close in prayer ask:

• for opportunities to laugh and march forth with mirth;

• God to give each participant the strength and courage to embrace celebration as a discipline;

• the Holy Spirit to speak to each person.

Where do you need to throw confetti?

Joyful ARE WE!

One of the best way to get joy, was to give it.

Sacred echos.

IDENTIFY THE FIRST STEP TO FIGHT BACK WITH JOY

✏️ THIS WEEK:

If you're following along in the book, read chapters ".004 The Biggest Myth About Joy," ".005 When You're Tearing Your Hair Out," and ".006 How to Throw the Best Party Ever" and dive into the five days of homework to prepare for the next gathering.

A few weeks ago, a package arrived in the mail from one of my best friends, Janella. Inside I found an elegant navy blue box with the following passage from Isaiah written in calligraphy on the top:

Those who hope in the LORD
will renew their strength.
They will soar on wings like eagles;
they will run and not grow weary,
they will walk and not be faint.
ISAIAH 40:31, NIV

Lifting the lid, I discovered a thick coffee mug with the word "Strength" written in large letters. Janella explained in a handwritten note that more than just a gift, this was her prayer for me.

Her thoughtfulness proved a beam of sunshine on a rough day. Her card and gift reminded me of her prayers and love.

Turning the box in my hand, something jangled. Two pieces of ceramic clanked in the box. I pressed my fingers along the bottom of the package and discovered that the handle of the mug had broken during shipping.

Tenderly holding the two shards next to the word "Strength" on the coffee mug, I busted out laughing. The irony wasn't lost on me.

In that moment, a broken "Strength" mug was the best gift anyone on the planet could give me. Why? Because it represented so much of what I was learning and experiencing through the hardships we were facing. Before the medical adversity I believed strength was found in hard work, diligence, discipline, and consistency. And those things do make us stronger— particularly when we invoke them at the gym.

Circle the things that make you feel stronger:

Health   Work   Appearance   Friendship

Diligence   Discipline   Laughter   Exercise

Consistency   Community   Faith   Hope

Where do you primarily derive your strength?

In things I do, and the more I do and succeed, the stronger I feel

I was finding new facets of strength among the shattered, broken, and crushed areas of my life. I was beginning to discover God's strength on the days I couldn't get out of bed, the afternoons I couldn't walk 10 feet without being winded, the mornings my emotional reserves were spent by 8 a.m.

Strength emerged amidst the rubble.

Which of the following have you found to be true in your own life? Place a check √ by all that apply.

❏ Strength isn't just found in giving but also in learning to receive well.
☑ Strength isn't just found in helping others but also in asking for help.
❏ Strength isn't just found in doing but also in being.

✚ BONUS ACTIVITY:

Spend time committing James 1:2-4 to memory this week. You'll find a flash card on page 193.

I had found all these statements to be true in my life. Some dimensions of God's strength can only be found in drinking from the cup of brokenness.

Perhaps this is what Paul had discovered when he asked God to remove the thorn in his flesh.

Rewrite 2 Corinthians 12:7-10 in your own words.

When we go through trials we are strengthed by the lord. Keeping us weak helps us to become strong.

What parallels do you see between how God responded to Paul's weaknesses and how He responds to yours?

When I am not humble and try to do everything myself, the hardships seem to pile on. But when I turn to God my load is lighter and I am stronger to deal w/ it

Throughout my medical treatment, my strength was zapped. I became more and more weak, and as I did, my life seemed to shrink. Everyday activities I once enjoyed became off limits. With a compromised immune system, I had to be careful to avoid chemicals, germs, and sunshine. Some days I went to the mall for a walk and got lapped by people 40 years older than me.

I grew frustrated. Yet defiance to my new limitations wasn't making anything or anyone better—including me. I spoke to a Christian counselor about how to deal with the laundry list of limitations I was now facing. He said the same word again and again: Accept.

Now, he wasn't saying I needed to accept the cancer. He agreed with me that we wanted every last evil cell out of my body. But I did need to accept the new limitations in my life and the reality that my life was different. Such acceptance opened my heart wider for meeting Christ in the midst of the difficult circumstances.

As I slowly came to terms with accepting my physical limitations, I was able to adapt. I could find ways to accomplish more with less and even let some things go completely. Accepting and adapting opened the door for me to depend more on Christ—in the tiniest of details—and provided me great strength.

ACCEPT + ADAPT + DEPEND = STRENGTH

 QUOTABLE:

"Beware of spending too much time looking back at what you once were when God wants you to become something you have never been."
—Oswald Chambers, evangelist and teacher[1]

My hunch is that you're facing some limitations of your own. Sometimes we choose our limitations, like developing a budget or starting a diet. But often our limitations choose us.

Somewhere along the way the energy we once felt pulse through our veins begins to wane. Pulling an all-nighter in college seems like a distant memory, a different version of ourselves. Our bodies demand more recovery time from us after a climb up the stairs, a long bike ride, a golf game, a Zumba class.

The limitation could rear its head in your workplace or in your ability to tutor your child in trigonometry. Perhaps it comes in the form of a physical injury that happened years ago.

What limitations or life restrictions are taking a toll on you right now? <u>Underline</u> all that apply.

Physical strength	Diet	Disease
Lack of energy	Clarity of mind	Recovery time
Crippling pain	Isolation	Aging
Finances	Size of home	Working vehicles
Addiction	Kids' schedules	Insomnia
Dwindling eyesight	Depression	Unemployment

(Circle) the limitation that is hardest for you right now. What makes it so difficult?

I've never forgotten the counselor's wisdom. His words fortified my determination to fight back with joy.

Just yesterday, I arrived home to a pile of dirty clothes on the floor of our bedroom. Everything in me wanted them clean, clean, clean. But my to-do list was far too long and my energy level registered at "0." I stared at the colorful clump of dirty laundry.

"Accept," I whispered to myself. "Accept."

In those choice syllables, I granted myself more than a permission slip to leave the laundry undone. I gave myself the time and space I needed to allow my body to heal.

I slipped on the wrinkly pajamas worn the night before and crawled into bed. I hadn't just accepted, I'd also adapted. In my old life, I would have loved to slip on fresh, hot-out-of-the-dryer pajamas after a long day. Now any pair of jammies would do.

The light clicked off, only 3:00 in the afternoon. The day before I felt angry that my body had turned on me so early. But now, as I followed this path of acceptance and adaptation, I accepted that I could no longer do everything. Instead, I needed to trust that God held everything under control. My mind calmed in the quiet. The last thing I remember before falling asleep was feeling ... well ... happy.

Through weakness, I am finding strength. In the process, I have stumbled onto one of the great paradoxes of faith.

Throughout Jesus' teaching, He reflected on the great reversals: The first will be last. In losing our lives, we find them. True strength is only found in weakness. We discover more when we have less.

Consider Jesus' magnum opus, the Sermon on the Mount. This teaching is marked by paradoxes (see Matt. 5:3-5). Each invites us to awaken to joy in the midst of difficulty. Jesus says that in the most trying times, we are actually blessed. In essence, Jesus says that the secret to a "blessed" life isn't what you'd first think. The Greek word used here, *makarios*, can also be translated as *happy*.

Which of the declarations of happiness or blessedness in Matthew 5:1-12 is most challenging to you?

having a pure heart

In the original language, the teaching bursts with alliteration:

- Happy are the poor (*ptochoi*) in spirit …

- Happy are those who mourn (*penthountes*) …

- Happy are the meek (*praeis*) …

From the poor to the persecuted, Jesus promised a bestowal of divine grace. Anchored to the realities of living in a broken world, the declarations of the Beatitudes burrow into the deepest levels of human desires—finding comfort, being fed, laying hold of justice, laughing, and experiencing a rich relationship with God.

Jesus said that when adversity knocks us off balance, it can reorient us to a more Godward, blessed life. Adversity has a way of shattering our illusions. It loosens our grip on self-sufficiency, independence, and invincibility. But once freed from the illusions, we can begin to assemble a new life, one marked by deeper encounters with each other and God. A simplicity of faith emerges as we put our trust wholly in Him. Our hearts crack open to a depth of happiness and joy we didn't know before.

Describe a time in your life when an illusion was shattered. How did the experience increase your dependence on God?

When I thought my marriage could be Repaired. My loneliness + struggles lead me to lean on God.

When you trust wholly in God, you will find more of the God-life and more God in your life than you could when you stood upright on your own. In those moments, when circumstance shoves you down, the list of limitations lengthens, and the battle grows fiery, rest assured. God will scoop you up extra tight. In His strong arms, you'll find joy.

In what kinds of situations does Paul learn to be content according to Philippians 4:11-13?

times of need

How has Paul learned to accept, adapt, and depend?

by find strength in God.

NOTABLE:

Throughout the New Testament, the Greek word *makarios* is often used to describe a person who is "happy" or "blessed." This is the word translated *blessed* throughout the Beatitudes. "Blessed are the poor in spirit, for theirs is the kingdom of heaven" (Matthew 5:3, NIV) can be understood as "happy" are the poor in spirit. Jesus promised the *makarios* life when He said, "If ye know these things, happy are ye if ye do them" (John 13:17, KJV).

How content are you in your life now? Mark your response on the continuum below:

●————————————————✗—————————————————●

I'm rarely content
in every situation.

I'm highly content
in every situation.

What is your biggest roadblock to being content in the situations you face?

Loosing weight

I continue to write myself permission slips to accept, adapt, and depend in daily life. This is what mine look like:

Permission Slips for Margaret

In the face of *limitations*, I give myself permission to:
accept, adapt, and depend.

In the face of *physical exhaustion*, I give myself permission to:
put down the to-do list and rest.

In the face of *feeling overwhelmed*, I give myself permission to:
graciously cancel and stay home.

In the face of *much to do*, I give myself permission to:
leave projects undone without feeling guilty

Now it's your turn. Create your own permission slips based on the limitations you're facing. Write how you will choose to accept, adapt, and depend on Christ.

Permission Slip for *Sandra*

In the face of *feeling to eat right*, I give myself permission to:
try again the next day
.

In the face of *feeling exhausted*, I give myself permission to:
to give myself a break + remove something from my to do.

In the face of _____, I give myself permission to:

_____

_____.

You and I have a choice. We can choose to rage against confines or determine to fight back with joy and create a more beautiful life within new limitations.

♥ **CLOSING PRAYER:** Ask God to help you process any losses or limitations in your life. Ask Him to give you the grace to accept, adapt, and depend on Him more.

DAY TWO

TAKE JOY, OH MY SOUL!

When it comes to worry, anxiety, and fear, I've noticed a pattern. They love midnight ambushes. In those dark, early hours of the morning, tiny concerns morph into gangly, blackened shadows. My mind begins ruminating on endless possibilities—none of them good—until I'm gripped by fear and anxiety.

Just last night I woke up at 1:12 a.m. I started thinking about an upcoming lunch with a new friend. What if we don't connect well? What if I don't know what to say? What if she doesn't like me? Negative thoughts fired through my mind, *Maybe you shouldn't do this. You won't have a good time. You should just cancel and stay home.* I soon grew fearful and defeated as I lay in bed, panicky.

➕ BONUS ACTIVITY:

Don't forget to continue adding moments when you've experienced joy from God to your Joy Bomb Journal.

Place a check √ beside each of the things that tend to ambush you during the midnight hours.

❑ Fear	☑ Insecurity	❑ Anxiety	❑ Panic
❑ Hopelessness	❑ Depression	❑ Discouragement	☑ Stress
❑ Frustration	❑ Failures	❑ Other :	

That midnight ambush reminded me that the way we talk to ourselves matters. All of us have that inner voice that offers a commentary on our lives, but so often the voice that speaks is harsh, unkind, and self-defeating.

Place a check √ beside the statements you have spoken to yourself.

❑ I'm a failure.	❑ I'm so dumb.
☑ They'll never like me.	❑ I'll never fit in.
❑ I might as well not try.	❑ I don't belong here.
❑ There's no way I could do that.	☑ I might as well give up.
☑ I'm a fake.	❑ I don't have a chance.

That voice doesn't just use words; it often projects images that are equally destructive. We can begin picturing ourselves failing or making mistakes. We may even imagine something bad happening to ourselves or those we love.

The impact of these negative words and images on our lives is profound, because they create a spiraling effect. The more we ruminate on negative and untrue statements about ourselves, the further we slip from the truth of what God thinks. And we fall into discouragement and depression. Joy slips away.

Perhaps this is no truer than in times of crisis or personal difficulty when the fears are no longer imaginary and vulnerabilities are exposed. That's when we need to be on extra high alert to the words and images we allow into our lives.

The Book of Proverbs reminds us that our words are serious business. They have the power to kill and give life. The syllables we utter yield two types of harvests: bitter poison or sweet fruit.

According to Proverbs 18:21, what kind of harvest are you bringing into your life with the words you speak to yourself?

the tongue has the power of life + death. Those who eat it well heal it's fruit

One of the most powerful ways to fight back with joy is to engage in less hurtful self-talk and more holy soul-talk. What is holy soul-talk?

Throughout the Bible, we find powerful statements that we can say to ourselves. Instead of speaking unkind and untrue things, we can take every thought captive, making it obedient to Christ (see 2 Cor. 10:4-5). One of the ways we do this is by believing what God says more than what we, circumstances, other people, or our feelings say. We can literally speak the truth of Scripture to ourselves.

In each of the following passages, the soul is directed toward an action. Circle the instruction for the soul in each passage.

March on, my soul; be strong!
JUDGES 5:21, NIV

My soul will rejoice in the LORD
and delight in his salvation.
PSALM 35:9, NIV

✚ BONUS ACTIVITY:
Dive deeper into the idea of soul-talk in Jennifer Rothschild's book, *Self Talk, Soul Talk: What to Say When You Talk to Yourself.*

As the deer pants for streams of water,
so my soul pants for you, my God.
PSALM 42:1, NIV

My soul thirsts for God, for the living God.
When can I go and meet with God?
PSALM 42:2, NIV

Why, my soul, are you downcast?
Why so disturbed within me?
Put your hope in God,
for I will yet praise him,
my Savior and my God.
PSALM 42:5, NIV

Praise the LORD, my soul,
and forget not all his benefits.
PSALM 103:2, NIV

Yes, my soul, find rest in God;
my hope comes from him.
PSALM 62:5, NIV

Return to your rest, my soul,
for the LORD has been good to you.
PSALM 116:7, NIV

QUOTABLE:

"A joyful heart makes a cheerful face, But when the heart is sad, the spirit is broken." — Proverbs 15:13, NASB

Do you see the power in each of these passages? We can literally direct our souls to be strong, rejoice in the Lord, thirst for God, put our hope in God, remember His goodness, and find rest in Him.

In those moments when you find yourself ruminating on negative thoughts and involved in harmful chatter, redirect your inner conversation toward God using the truth of Scripture.

It's amazing how often I find myself slipping into negative self-talk. I sink into a stinky pit thinking, *This will never end, and I'll never get through this.*

In these moments, I discovered the power of engaging in holy soul-talk and clinging to the truth of God's Word. On the weakest days, I cling to the declaration of Judges 5:21 (NIV):

> March on, my soul; be strong!

Sometimes I say it to myself a hundred times in a single day just to trudge through. On the days that I'm tempted to doubt God's faithfulness, I ground myself in the truth of Psalm 103:2 (NIV):

QUOTABLE:
"How my spirit rejoices in God my Savior!"
—Luke 1:47, NLT

> Praise the LORD, my soul, and forget not his benefits.

These passages have become lifelines. One of the reasons they are so powerful and effective for me is because of their brevity. They are easy to remember. Simple to command. Quick to reground me.

But these aren't the only ones. Sometimes, when I imagine a dark scenario, I need to refocus my attention. That's when I turn to Psalm 23 and imagine myself with God as my Shepherd—leading me beside still waters and restoring my soul. This scriptural imagery allows me to regain a sense of peace and trust in God.

One of the passages I cling to most tightly is Psalm 27:13-14 (NASB):

> I would have despaired unless I had believed that I would see the
> goodness of the LORD
> in the land of the living.
> Wait for the LORD;
> be strong and let your heart take courage;
> yes, wait for the LORD.

What commands are inherent to the soul in this passage?

be strong, take courage

This Scripture, along with the others, has become one of the ways I fight back with joy. I use God's Word to beat back discouragement and depression. These passages strengthen my inner resolve to take joy, O my soul!

SOMETIMES YOU HAVE TO POKE HOLES IN THE DARKNESS UNTIL IT BLEEDS LIGHT.

What passage do you use to speak life into your soul during difficult times? What commands are inherent to the soul in your passage? If you haven't used this practice yet, which passage will you commit to memory today?

As I learn to speak Scripture to my soul during times of doubt, fear, or anxiety, I retrain my mind and heart to see myself as God does. I will probably have to repeat those same passages a bazillion times over, but each time I do, I shift my eyes to the truth of Scripture. Worries shrink. Frustration fades. Joy returns.

💚 **CLOSING PRAYER:** Invite God into the midnight ambushes. Ask God to wash you with the truth of how He sees you and your circumstances. Ask for renewed strength as you switch from self-talk to soul-talk.

DAY THREE

EMBRACE CELEBRATION AS A DISCIPLINE

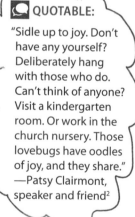

I'm hesitant to go to parties where I don't know anyone. I feel nervous and unsure. What if I don't have anyone to talk to? What if I don't have anything in common with the people there? What if I'm not dressed appropriately? Sometimes the hardest part of parties is leaving my house.

Once Leif coaxes me out the door, I usually have the best time. Though there may be a few awkward moments, it's amazing how often I'll meet fascinating people, laugh lots, and sample super tasty food.

When it comes to attending a party where you don't know anyone, which of the following statements best describes you?

❏ I'll be ready in five.   ❏ Can I bring a friend?
☑ That sounds scary.   ❏ I have to wash the dog tonight.
❏ Oh! What's on the menu?   ❏ What can I bring?

One of the facets of God's character that I adore is that He loves to throw a good party. Throughout the Old Testament, God established seven annual feasts to be celebrated: Passover, The Feast of Unleavened Bread, The Feast of First Fruits, The Feast of Weeks, The Feast of Trumpets, The Day of Atonement, and The Feast of Tabernacles.

Each of these Jewish feasts is associated with Israel's agricultural seasons. These celebrations reminded the Israelites each year of God's goodness—including His protection and provision. They also foreshadow the redemptive work of Jesus.

But partying isn't just reserved to the Old Testament.

The Gospel of John describes the first miracle of Jesus' earthly ministry: turning water into wine at a wedding celebration (see John 2:1-10). And when the prodigal son returns home, the father throws a huge party (see Luke 15:22-25).

To what does Jesus compare the kingdom of heaven in Luke 14:15-24?

a feast

Why were the Pharisees so frustrated with Jesus according to Luke 7:34?

because he was eating + drinking

Based on Luke 7:36-50, where was Jesus when He was anointed for His burial?

dinner at the Pharisee's house

Where did Jesus eat His final meal with His disciples according to Matthew 26:17-30?

at a man's house over dinner.

What does Jesus say in Luke 15:5-7 about what happens when a sinner repents?

there will be rejoicing in heaven

Read Revelation 19:6-9. What party is promised to those who follow Jesus?

the wedding supper of the lamb

God commanded the Israelites to gather throughout the year and celebrate His wonders and provision. The pilgrimages involved weren't always easy or convenient. Yet through these holy days people tasted, saw, declared, and remembered God's goodness. These festivals reoriented God's people toward His presence and faithfulness. And sometimes we need to be reminded and reoriented, too.

QUOTABLE:

"We Christians are the speakers of light. We are the proclaimers of joy. Wherever we go, we are the mascots of the gospel, the imagers of the infinitely creative Father, and the younger brothers and sisters of the humbled and triumphant Word. We speak in this world on behalf of the One who made up lightning and snowflakes and eggs."
—N. D. Wilson, author[3]

Most of the battlefields in life force us to duck for cover in the miry trenches. As soon as the sun dips below the horizon, the cold dampness descends and gnaws away at our resolve. We find ourselves dwelling in darkness, second-guessing if we'll ever escape.

But Scripture reveals that even the faintest expressions of celebration can infuse us with strength and fill us with hope. Joy begets joy. Each act, no matter how small, is an outward expression of an inward trust in God's ability to meet our needs. When we choose to celebrate, we demonstrate faith in God. That's why sometimes we must:

EMBRACE CELEBRATION AS A DISCIPLINE.

Practicing joy during disastrous times may look silly, ludicrous, even inappropriate to the untrained eye. But celebration never denies the harsh realities of the situation. It demonstrates that you can look beyond the immediate situation and see God's perspective. You aren't throwing a party because of the loss, tragedy, or pain, but in spite of it. You are choosing to rejoice in the Lord, the God of your salvation, the God your Savior. God is to be celebrated in times of feast and in times of famine.

Moments of celebration, especially in times of great adversity, require faith. If joy is the abiding sense of God's fierce love for us, then celebration asks us to act on it by practicing an abundance mentality in times of scarcity.

In what area of your life do you most need to embrace celebration as a discipline right now as an act of trusting God despite circumstances?

Despite my children all leaving home

NOTABLE:

"Embrace celebration as a discipline" means that you can squint beyond the present situation and glimpse the bigger picture from God's perspective. You don't throw confetti because of your situation. You rejoice in the Lord in spite of your situation. You activate joy by celebrating God whether you're in a time of lack or a time of plenty.

What will you do to throw some confetti this week?

embrace the quiet & prepare for celebrating via lunch @ work

One of the practical ways that Leif and I embraced celebration as a discipline was by showing up to doctor's appointments with party food. One week, Leif made his famous black-eyed pea hummus with crunchy pita chips. Another he experimented with ranch dip complemented by fresh-cut vegetables. We'd bring fresh fruit, gooey chocolate chip cookies, just-out-of-the-oven brownies, and more. The act of bringing yummy snacks to the staff that served us created points of connection and made the appointments a lot more fun.

What's your favorite go-to party food or drink?

artichoke dip
Tiramisu

+ BONUS ACTIVITY:

We'd love to know your go-to recipes for party food. Share yours at *facebook.com/ margaretfeinberg*.

+ BONUS ACTIVITY: WHIP UP YUMMY BALLOON OF JOY COOKIES
(Recipe makes 4 dozen)

COOKIE INGREDIENTS:
· 2 ¾ cups all-purpose flour (use your favorite type of flour)
· 1 teaspoon baking soda
· ½ teaspoon baking powder
· ¼ cup nonfat Greek yogurt
· ½ cup applesauce
· 1 ½ cup white sugar
· 1 egg
· 1 teaspoon vanilla extract
· 24 lollipop sticks (Popsicle™ sticks work, too!)

ICING INGREDIENTS:
· Your favorite white pre-made icing/frosting
· Food coloring in your favorite colors

DIRECTIONS:
1. Preheat oven to 375 degrees.
2. Mix dry ingredients in medium mixing bowl.
3. Mix wet ingredients in large mixing bowl.
4. While mixing, combine dry ingredients into wet ingredients until fully combined.
5. Scoop out 1-inch rolls of dough onto ungreased baking sheets.
6. Insert lollipop or popsicle sticks ¼ into the cookie dough.
7. Bake until golden brown (about 8-10 minutes).
8. While the cookies are baking, whip up your favorite pre-made icing/frosting with food coloring. You can have all the same color or different bowls of frosting with different colors.
9. When cookies are done baking, let them cool for 30 minutes before frosting.
10. Share your Balloon of Joy Cookies with friends, neighbors, and coworkers to pass along the joy.

+ BONUS ACTIVITY:

Look online for a reason to smile. Check out 30 delightful photos of children from around the world playing at *www.boredpanda.com/ happy-children-playing*.

The ways we embrace celebration as a discipline will vary. For some, it may mean bringing a bouquet of flowers to a sick friend, wearing bright colors on a particularly dreary day, mowing a neighbor's lawn, or leaving encouraging notes on strangers' doorsteps. Maybe the celebration is something you need to start practicing in your own home.

Jane had flowers from her garden that needed pruning. Instead of tossing them away, she left them on doorsteps around her whole neighborhood. She admitted that sometimes she rang the doorbell and ran, so her gift would be in secret. When the neighbors opened the door, a fresh bouquet of flowers awaited them.

Her husband, Harold, delivered the rest of the bouquets to a nursing home—the same nursing home where his dad had passed away a few months before.

Who have you been struggling to get along with?

How can you resolve to respond with joy and celebration no matter what during your next interaction with this person?

✚ BONUS ACTIVITY:
Check the back of your closet, the top shelf of your pantry, and under your bed. What have you been saving for a special day? Make today the day. Use the special occasion dishes. Drink from those fancy glasses. Splash on your best perfume. Instead of saving special joys for "one day," why not make one happen today?

Sometimes it's difficult to throw confetti in the midst of what you're fighting. It may feel impossible to blow a party horn among much discontent. Yet such merrymaking reawakens our souls to God. And believe it or not, frolicking can even become a prayer for God to renew our sense of divine delight.

The smallest festivities of the heart can expand our capacity to enjoy and obey God. They remind us to search for God in all things and declare His goodness on the darkest days. They ready us to receive the fullness of gifts and mercies of grace.

♥ **CLOSING PRAYER:** Sometimes we just don't feel like celebrating, but we know that the joy of the Lord is our strength. Ask God to give you the resolve to begin acting on joy even when you don't feel like it.

DISCOVER JOY
IN THE MOURNING

We all have reasons to grieve. Sometimes the source of grief centers on a diagnosis, a divorce, a death of a loved one. Other times the source of grief is subtler—a move to a new town, kids leaving for college, letting go of a lifelong dream.

In the wake of my diagnosis, I had so much to grieve. Overnight it felt like I had lost my health, my strength, my life. The months of treatment took a heavy toll on our relationships, our vitality, our finances.

Yet I had never been taught how to mourn. Perhaps you haven't either.

On the continuum below, mark how much you understand about mourning:

I know how to   I don't know how
mourn loss.   to mourn loss.

NOTABLE:

Grief is derived from the Latin verb meaning *to be burdened*. For some, grief can feel like a heavy burden. *Mourning* is derived from the Latin verb meaning *be anxious*. Mourning is a process of remembering what was lost and provides a way for our bodies, minds, and hearts to metabolize loss.

Mourning isn't something our culture acknowledges or engages in well. We may be tempted to tell ourselves the loss isn't a big deal; if we ignore the pain it will fade away; or we just need to get on with life. We may even tell ourselves that because of our faith, mourning is unnecessary.

Yet the Bible acknowledges grief as a God-given response to loss. Even God grieves.

What does the Father grieve over in Psalm 95:11?

People whose heart goes astray

What does the Son grieve over in John 11:35-38?

Lazarus' death

What does the Spirit grieve over in Ephesians 4:30-31?

unwholesome talk, bitterness anger

Jesus even describes those who mourn or those who work through the process of grief as "blessed."

Happy are those who mourn;
God will comfort them!
MATTHEW 5:4, GNT

How have you experienced this blessing in your own life?

Being around family after a loved one passes, feeling the joy of being

As followers of Jesus, we are called to mourn with those who mourn (see Rom. 12:15). But it's hard to mourn well with others if we never learn to mourn our losses.

Why is mourning so important? When we don't learn how to mourn or allow ourselves the opportunity to mourn, our bandwidth for feeling narrows. We may not feel as much pain, but we also short-circuit our ability to experience joy.

Psalm 30:5 tells us that joy comes in the morning, but what I've discovered is that:

JOY COMES IN THE MOURNING.

On the continuums below, mark how much you've been able to mourn the losses in your life:

●————X————————————————●
I've mourned   I haven't mourned
the larger losses in life.   the larger losses in life.

●————————————————X————●
I've mourned   I haven't mourned
the smaller losses in life.   the smaller losses in life.

QUOTABLE:

"A state of emotion always comes between the knowledge and the act … God intended that truth should move us to moral action. The mind receives ideas, mental pictures of things as they are. These excite the feelings and these in turn move the will to act in accordance with the truth … Be sure that human feelings can never be completely stifled. If they are forbidden their normal course, like a river they will cut another channel through the life and flow out to curse and ruin and destroy."
—A. W. Tozer, author[4]

Our spiritual vitality depends on our ability to mourn the larger and lesser losses of life. Place a check ✓ mark beside the losses you've experienced and mourned. Then (circle) the losses you are either still mourning or have never taken time to mourn.

- ☑ Death of a loved one
- ☐ Infertility
- ☑ Miscarriage
- ☐ Childhood abuse
- ☐ An absent parent
- ☐ Bankruptcy
- ☐ Job loss
- ☐ Foreclosure
- ☐ Abusive spouse
- ☐ Terminal illness
- ☐ Alcoholic parent
- ☐ Lawsuit
- ☐ Embezzlement
- ☐ Empty nest

- ☐ Loss of youth
- ☐ Physical limitation
- ☐ Friends who moved away
- ☐ Loss of pet
- ☐ Loss of identity
- ☐ Loss of achievement
- ☐ Aging
- ☑ Break-up
- ☑ Necessary ending of a friendship
- ☐ Loss of freedom after becoming a parent
- ☐ Other: _____

Pause for a moment and ask the Holy Spirit what else in your past or present you've never taken the time to mourn. Write what comes to mind below.

my unborn child

Every loss is important. In my own journey, some of the lesser losses were the most difficult. For example, the loss of my hair during chemotherapy evoked incredible grief—even more so than the removal of my breasts. Now, logically, that seems ridiculous. One would grow back. Yet I had to give myself permission to grieve all the losses—no matter how small.

One of the places where I found comfort and the courage to begin mourning was in studying the Jewish rites surrounding mourning. The protocol behind the Jewish practices is meant to help those who mourn find meaning.

The Torah teaches Jews to bury their dead quickly. This is based on the command to not "let the body remain all night" (Deut. 21:23). Following the funeral, mourners enter into a practice known as "sitting shivah" or "sitting seven," as an intensive weeklong mourning period following the death of an immediate relative. The time is marked by austerity.

Who sat shivah with Job after his great loss according to Job 2:11-13?

his 3 friends

What did they say to Job during this time?

not a word

Mourners do not bathe or shower. Men do not shave. Women do not wear makeup. Nothing freshly laundered may be worn. Married couples refrain from sex. Mourners sit low to the ground. One doesn't leave the house except for Sabbath services. Studying the Torah is considered too great a pleasure for this time. The only texts permitted are Job, Lamentations, portions of Jeremiah, and the Rabbinic laws of mourning.

All the mirrors in the house must be covered to honor the dignity of the deceased since beauty and ornamentation are considered an insult to a decomposing body. The practice also gives permission to mourners to look and feel miserable and to greet guests with puffy eyes and messy hair. Society heralds vanity as a way of life, but covering the household mirrors grounds mourners in the truth that appearance is irrelevant, time isn't to be wasted, and now is the chance to get priorities straight.

A closer look at the laws of shivah reveals the command for the mourners to behave as if they're dead. With every distraction removed, the mourners must face the loss for seven whole days. They must endure exhaustion, boredom, and a barrage of emotions. Shivah leaves no exits for denial or shrugging off the loss.

Sitting shivah reminded me of the great importance of mourning. Grieving wasn't something to be shoved away or avoided but instead sought out and embraced for the healing it brings.

Sitting shivah creates space for quiet to process our losses with God.

That's what I needed more than anything to mourn well—time and space and silence and permission to let the tears fall. For me, pockets of mourning appeared in the most unexpected places. I wept in the movie theater during a matinee. One evening the dam of tears broke while watching the sun cast its final vibrant shadows over the mountains. Tears flowed during times of study and reflection, on the hour-plus long daily hikes, in the darkness of the bedroom. Many mornings Leif and I sat nestled on the couch beside each other having the gravest, most difficult conversations any couple can ever have. We often ended by weeping in each other's arms.

4 GUIDELINES TO MOURNING WELL

1 **GIVE YOURSELF PERMISSION TO MOURN THE LOSS.**
Welcome and accept the emotions you're feeling. Rather than try to stuff away the sadness, anger, guilt, or fear, welcome the multitude of emotions. Tell God what you're feeling. You may want to do this verbally or through a journal or artwork.

2 **ACCEPT THAT YOUR GRIEF IS UNIQUE.** We all mourn in our own way and on our own timetable. The process of grief has several stages including shock, numbness, and denial (see Mark 8:31-32), anger (see Job 10:9), bargaining (see Isa. 38:1-22), and acceptance (see Phil. 1:12,21-24), but this isn't a linear path. Some days you'll feel shock, then jump to anger, then denial, and back again.

3 **KNOW THAT YOU DON'T HAVE TO DO THIS ON YOUR OWN.**
Reach out to a group of friends, family members, a support group, your pastor, or a Christian counselor who can help you process what you're going through.

4 **RECOGNIZE YOUR GRIEF TRIGGERS.** You may find particular dates, holidays, events, or even music can trigger sadness. Develop strategies for how to best approach these places, times, or situations.

What guideline would you add to this list?

It's ok to take the time, to wallow in it for a bit

For more than a year, I've been learning to mourn. I find comfort in recognizing God's response to our grief. When we choose to mourn, we do not mourn alone. God is with us.

 BONUS ACTIVITY:

Rose-Lynn Fisher photographed 100 tears through a standard light microscope. The tears of happiness, grief, and hope look very different. Check out "The Topography of Tears" images at *rose-lynnfisher.com*.

NOTABLE:

In Rabbinic literature, a sword represented mourning. The vivid imagery suggested a loss could strike deep at any time. During the first three days of mourning, the image of a sword was raised above a mourner's shoulder. Through day 7, the sword could approach the bereaved from the corner of the room. Those who suffered through loss of a loved one could expect the sword could pass him or her on the street until the end of day 30. And the sword was likely to strike any family member throughout the full year. This imagery reminds us that moments of mourning can hit us at any time—long after the loss has occurred.

What is God's response to our mourning according to the following passages?

Psalm 56:8: *Record it*

Hebrews 4:15: *God has been through the same things as us*

Isaiah 65:19: *delight will come, he will turn us around*

I recently asked my friends on Facebook what they've found helpful in mourning:

"Don't isolate." —Brendan

"Reminding myself that the reason it is so hard is because there was so much love." —Teresa

"Give yourself permission to cry. Know that's it's OK to break down. Just don't unpack there and stay." —Hannah

"I've had five miscarriages. It's a unique kind of loss because there is nothing tangible to point to. We decided to name our unborn babies and then had a plaque made with their names and the meanings. It has helped us to give ourselves a tangible reminder." —Kjerstin

"After my grandmother passed two years ago, every time the clock was on a repetitive number, I would tell her I loved her. Example: 11:11, 2:22, etc. It helped me." —Sheryl

"Cookies, walks, songs, honoring the person by drawing how I see them. Did I say cookies?" —Keri

"Give yourself permission to not be on your mental A-game and to fully feel what you feel as you feel it. Grief isn't a linear process, and it's not really controllable. It's something we get through, not over. Some people may be able to empathize; some friends may not be able to cope with seeing you grieve, or they may not know what to do or how to handle it. It's normal; just find one or two people who can empathize and be present with you. Nobody gets to tell you what your grief journey looks like or how long it will take. Fall forward toward healthy ways of dealing with grief, don't allow yourself to make huge life-changing decisions within the first year if at all possible." —Michelle

Underline any phrases in the statements above that might be personally helpful to you.

One of the best resources I've found to help process mourning is a Christian counselor. This person has helped me recognize which stage of grieving I'm in and process through the pain, anger, and guilt.

Would you be willing to talk to a Christian counselor about the areas of loss you're dealing with in your life right now? Who can you call for a counselor recommendation?

If needed el would.
My church has the resources

A second resource that has helped me work through my grief is using a journal to talk openly to God about what I'm feeling. One of the best exercises for me was a practice in which I spoke to God about the grief, and then I invited God to speak to me about what the grief was doing in my life.

I'm going to take a huge risk and share a very tender, private moment from my journal.

Dear God,

Some days the grief seems more than I can bear. The losses too many to tally. The weight too heavy. The pain too piercing. The scars too deep. The tears refuse to stop flowing.

I choose to receive this grieving, this process of mourning as a gift from You. You can use our grief to speak to us, to cleanse us, to renew us, and to heal us. Father, what are You trying to say to me through this grief? I want to mourn and mourn well.

Much love,
Margaret

BONUS ACTIVITY:

Need help finding a Christian counselor in your area? Visit *aacc. net/resources/find-a-counselor/* for a list of accredited Christian counselors near you.

> "Praise be to the God and Father of our Lord Jesus Christ, the Father of compassion and the God of all comfort, who comforts us in all our troubles, so that we can comfort those in any trouble with the comfort we ourselves receive from God."
> —2 Corinthians 1:3-4, NIV

> "So do not fear, for I am with you; do not be dismayed, for I am your God. I will strengthen you and help you; I will uphold you with my righteous right hand."
> —Isaiah 41:10, NIV

> "When you pass through the waters, I will be with you; and when you pass through the rivers, they will not sweep over you. When you walk through the fire, you will not be burned; the flames will not set you ablaze." —Isaiah 43:2, NIV

> "My comfort in my suffering is this: Your promise preserves my life." —Psalm 119:50, NIV

Dear Margaret,

You don't have to carry this grief or burden on your own. I welcome all those who are weary and heavy burdened to come to Me (Matt. 11:28). On the days the grief seems too much, call on Me. Remember that I will never resist a broken or contrite heart (Ps. 51:17). Draw near to me and I will draw near to you (Jas. 4:8). Remember that you do not serve one who cannot sympathize with your weaknesses (Heb. 4:15).

Allow the mourning to run its course. Some days you'll feel like you're taking steps forward, other days you'll feel like you're taking steps backward. Some days you'll feel tired. Some days your energy will be renewed. Through this process, I'm going to reveal lesser priorities in your life and expand your ability to show compassion to others. Know that I am with you every step of the way (Matt. 28:20). And I am the one who promises to wipe every tear from your eye (Rev. 21:4).

Your Loving Father

Now I want to ask you to bravely be willing to do the same. Will you take a few moments and write a letter to God about the grief in your heart? Let Him know what you're feeling—your frustrations, your range of emotions, your hopes, and your fears.

Dear God,

Some days the grief seems …

I am alone and all have left me. I know my children are doing better things, but I miss them so much. Help me to process this + be better for them. And use this time to Strengthen My marriage

Much love,
Sandra

"I consider that our present sufferings are not worth comparing with the glory that will be revealed in us."
—Romans 8:18, NIV

"Those who sow in tears shall reap with shouts of joy!" —Psalm 126:5, ESV

Prayerfully consider how God wants to answer your concern. Write any thoughts or Bible passages that come to mind as you journal a response.

Dear _____ (your name),

Thank you for being honest about your grief. …

"Humble yourselves, therefore, under God's mighty hand, that he may lift you up in due time. Cast all your anxiety on him because he cares for you." —1 Peter 5:6-7, NIV

"For he has not despised or scorned the suffering of the afflicted one; he has not hidden his face from him but has listened to his cry for help." —Psalm 22:24, NIV

Your Loving Father

The process of mourning takes time. But as we learn to mourn our losses, we learn to mourn the losses of others with more compassion, grace, and love.

As you read through the following activities, circle the one that you will commit to try in your journey of mourning.

- **Keep a journal. Writing down your thoughts and feelings every day can provide a healthy means of recovery. Consider starting with the date of the entry then write or draw what you're feeling. Be completely honest and share with God what you're thinking, experiencing, and feeling.**
- **Set apart a time to cry. The depth of our loss and pain can bring us to tears. You may find it helpful to set apart 20-30 minutes each day just to have a good cry. Allow those tears to cleanse you. And as the weeks pass, you may notice yourself needing less time for the tears.**
- **Write a letter to your loss. It can be helpful to write a letter to a lost loved one, a lost object, a lost job—anything where there's unfinished business and closure is needed. These letters aren't meant to be mailed. They are to provide a safe place for deep, honest, emotional release.**
- **Consider writing a lament. Write about the pain, loss, and suffering and cry out to God as your source of hope and healing. Consider using Psalm 13 as a lament to guide you.**

My hope and prayer is that you will be courageous and take the grief you're feeling to God. Invite Him into your process of mourning. May you experience the comfort of the Holy Spirit and the healing that only God can bring.

♥ **CLOSING PRAYER:** Sometimes our losses are more than we can bear, but they are never more than God can bear. Ask Him to give you the strategies to mourn well so that you may find healing and wholeness and become a source of comfort to others.

DAY FIVE

TOSS ANCHORS INTO THE FUTURE

During times of personal crisis and difficulty, it's easy to get stuck. The adversity we're facing becomes all-consuming. It draws our attention, our resources, our emotional reserves, our everything until we're no longer moving forward in life.

Soon after the diagnosis, Leif and I discovered that almost all our time and energy were directed toward battling the disease. We spent anywhere from 20-30 hours a week at the hospital and at various doctor appointments. Our free time was spent researching the disease, insurance battles, and proper protocols for treatment. This went on until we woke up one day and realized that the only thing in our lives seemed to be the adversity we were facing.

While this is common for people in crisis, we knew we needed something more. Something to look forward to besides another drive to the hospital. Something to talk about with friends other than the medical updates. Something that would breathe life into our souls and joy into our hearts. We needed to dream about the future again.

That's when I found inspiration and encouragement from the life of Paul.

Slavery had long been practiced in the Greco-Roman world. Some were born into it; others entered through unpaid debt. Still others were kidnapped and taken against their will. The punishment for runaways included death. Those permitted to live endured barbaric torture including branding on the face, encasement in an iron collar, the breaking of both legs.

Onesimus knew the consequences for becoming a runaway all too well.

Yet he ran hard and fast anyway. I imagine the plot he rehearsed in his mind for months came together like a scene from *Ocean's Eleven*. I imagine him even pocketing some of his master's wealth to pay for his getaway to Rome.

Somewhere along the escape route Onesimus bumps into Paul and discovers Christ. The fugitive's life is unraveling and coming together at the same time.

The fledgling follower begins sharing his past with Paul. Their friendship soon grows deep. Over long meals and lengthy discussions, Paul pieces together the nitty-gritty of Onesimus's story. One particular detail leaves Paul spellbound: His new friend didn't just run away and steal from any master; he ran away and stole from Philemon, one of Paul's close friends.

If, even for the briefest of moments, Paul felt caught in the cross hairs, he never shows it. Instead, he advocates for forgiveness and mercy. He appeals to Philemon in the form of a personal letter to tally the slave's debt as his own, encouraging him to embrace Onesimus as a free man and brother in Christ. This is no small request.

On a personal level, Paul is willing to risk his relationship with Philemon to help Onesimus. But Paul also knows his appeal will become of great interest for the other churches. If Christianity could work in a sticky situation, a tough impasse like this one, then it could work anywhere.

Paul, Philemon, Onesimus, the church, and all of Christianity had much at stake in Philemon's response.[7]

Read the Book of Philemon (don't worry, it's a quick read). How would you describe Paul's tone throughout the letter?

What strikes you as significant about the way Paul makes his request?

> *It is loving but confident. Not an order, but he expects compliance*

Unlike Paul's other letters, he doesn't lean into weighty arguments of the law or history. Instead, he draws on the bonds of friendship. Paul approaches Philemon by using the terms of endearment "dear friend" and "fellow worker."

Paul commends Philemon for his love of others and faith in Christ, and he prays that the partnership will continue to deepen and grow through work that's being done. Paul prays that the "fellowship of your faith" (Philem. 1:6, NASB) will lead to an understanding of all that is good in the companionship of the other believers.

What's extraordinary about Paul's appeal is that he does it all from prison! A man behind bars pleads on behalf of a runaway. Enslaved because of the gospel, Paul advocates for a law-breaker. Though he sees the outline of his dark cell and the prison guards every day, he chooses to look beyond to the possibilities. He continues to serve God, love others, and even look toward the future.

Write Philemon 1:22 in your own words:

> *I have faith and ask you to pray, then I know I will be released*

In the letter to Philemon, it's easy to overlook this gem. But do you see what Paul is doing? He's throwing an anchor of hope into the future. He's declaring that even though he might be behind bars today, he trusts God to bring freedom tomorrow. That belief expresses itself in an action—asking that a room be readied.

In my life, I recognized the need to begin tossing out anchors. Though it didn't feel like the challenges we were facing were ever going to end, we began dreaming into the future.

Where there is no vision, the people perish.
PROVERBS 29:18, KJV

How have you found this to be true in your life?

If I didn't have something to look forward to, it would be difficult to get out of bed

The word "perish" in this passage describes fruit past its prime. Instead of ripening, the fruit is rotting. When we throw anchors into the future by planning activities and dreaming, we regain vision and restore perspective. This practice allows us to play offense instead of defense. My friend, Mark, likes to say, "You start dying when you have nothing worth living for. You start living when you find something worth dying for."

Tossing anchors into the future begins with simple, everyday actions that are within our grasp. One of the first things I did was purchase paint. We'd long needed an update on the peachy, flesh-colored walls in our bedroom. With the help of friends we enjoyed a slate grey with white trim makeover. Something as simple as fresh paint became a hope-filled expression of the future we were going to enjoy together.

What is one change you've been meaning to make around your house that would bring you joy but wouldn't take much time or money to accomplish?

Cleaning out a closet or cabinets.

Leif and I began to look for opportunities to place fun events on the calendar. Inviting friends over to dinner. Planning an afternoon at a local art exhibit. Scoping out tickets to an outdoor concert. Each of these activities became something that shifted our focus from the long, all-consuming days in the medical facilities toward events that filled us with life, hope, and joy.

Leif dreamed for years of making the ultimate escape from Alcatraz, the historic island prison located in the bay off San Francisco. He signed up for the 1.5 mile swimming competition known as "Alcatraz Sharkfest" a year before the event. Just registering opened a gateway of dreaming together about the trip and sharing a fun getaway with friends. It also offered a healthy outlet to connect with the local swimming community, improve his health, and have something to talk about other than the crisis we were facing.

How good are you at throwing joyful anchors into your future? Mark your response on the continuum below:

I throw joyful anchors
into the future on a regular basis.

I need to be more
intentional about throwing
joyful anchors into the future.

List five joyful anchors you could toss into your future right now.

1 A vacation
2 Studying or school for a new career
3 planning a visit to Alaska/Madison
4 make a date with friends
5 Tour Arizona or Grand Canyon / Vegas

We enjoyed throwing anchors so much that we sat down and created a dream list of activities to do, places to visit, and people to meet that may never happen but are fun to conjure up. Here's a snapshot of some items on our dream list:

Take a hot air balloon ride

Stay in an ice hotel

Surf with my dad

Hand out samples at Costco

Take an RV trip in the northeast

Go on a cruise

Visit the Grand Canyon

Listen to a Brooklyn Tabernacle concert live

Visit Mount Rushmore

~~Reconnect with an old friend~~

Visit New Zealand

~~Make marshmallows from scratch~~

Go into space

Watch a Broadway show

So far we've only been able to cross a few items off our dream list. But what a joy it's been!

Now a dream list is just that, dreaming. You may not be able to cross everything off your list in your lifetime, but in dreaming you allow yourself to toss anchors into the future and engage in alternate possibilities. For example, I may never get to travel to space, but I can spend a day at the planetarium, admire photos from the Hubble telescope online, and take time to tour Kennedy Space Center if we ever find ourselves in Florida.

Making, keeping, and reflecting on this list has become an opportunity to dream and pray about the future and the possibilities God may have for us.

Have you ever made a joy-filled dream list or bucket list? If so, pull it out and reread it right now. If not, you will have the opportunity to start your dream list today.

 QUOTABLE:

"So that by God's will I may come to you with joy and be refreshed in your company."
—Romans 15:32, ESV

WHEN IT COMES TO MAKING A DREAM LIST, HERE ARE A FEW TIPS TO KEEP IN MIND:

1 **BEGIN WITH PRAYER.** Ask God about the dreams He has for you. What does He want to accomplish in and through you? What longings has He placed in your heart?

2 **CONSIDER DIFFERENT CATEGORIES.** Think about your family, experiences, physical goals, and travel. Recognize that each of these can have a spiritual dimension.

3 **WRITE DOWN SPECIFICS.** If you don't write down your dream list, you may not notice opportunities God has placed before you.

4 **SHARE YOUR DREAMS WITH OTHERS.** Talking about your dreams and goals with others may help you discover new additions for your list. You may find friends who share the same desires, and you can work together to accomplish those goals and celebrate God's goodness and provision along the way.

Write Habakkuk 2:2 in your own words in the space below.

Write it down so it can happen! make a plan

Why is following this principle important?

If you don't plan or make a goal, how will it get done.

If you've never made a dream list, will you take a few moments to prayerfully dream right now? What do you want to do most in life? Whom do you want to reconnect with? Where do you want to visit? What skill do you want to learn? Make a list of 10 joy-filled dreams in the space below.

My Joy-Filled Dream List: It would bring me joy to …

1 *learn a language*
2 *make art*
3 *visit lake*
4 *travel to visit mom*
5 *work w/ babies*
6 *learn bead making*
7 *go on a safari*
8
9
10

Leif and I continue to add to our dream list with each "National Geographic" show we watch, vacation picture we admire on Facebook, and interesting article we read. And joy happens as we cast anchors into the future and allow ourselves to dream. Our hearts awaken and eyes widen in wonder as we look up and out, beyond our circumstances.

SESSION FOUR

A SIDE OF JOY NO ONE TALKS ABOUT

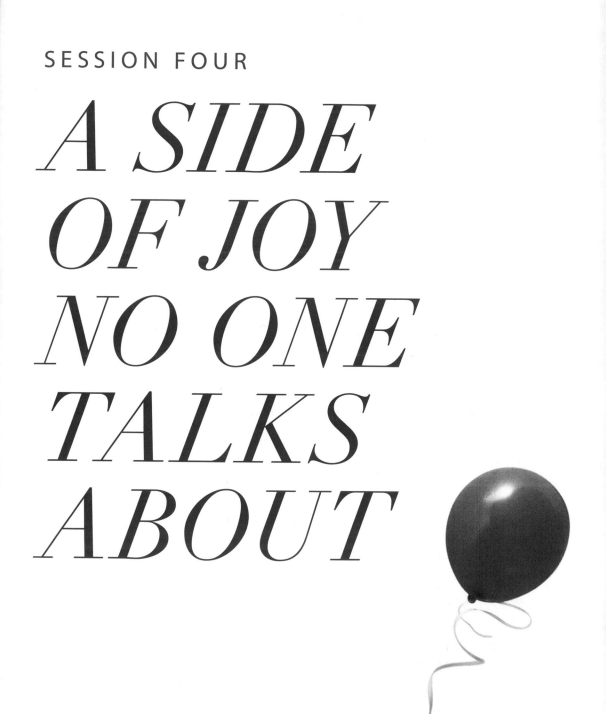

GROUP GETTING STARTED: (10-15 minutes)

SESSION FOUR:
A SIDE OF JOY NO ONE TALKS ABOUT

💬 HOMEWORK GROUP DISCUSSION

1. Share with the group three moments you recorded in your Joy Bomb Journal on page 168 in which you encountered gifts and joys from God this week.

2. From your Day One homework, what is one illusion you've had shattered by crisis? How has losing that illusion made you more dependent on God? *Pg. 78*

3. How did you embrace celebration as a discipline as described in your Day Three homework? What was the result? *86*

4. What is one thing you realized you needed to mourn from Day Four? In what ways are you learning to mourn the loss? *91*

5. Share three items on your joy-filled dream list from your Day Five work. *103*

🔗 EXPERIENTIAL ACTIVITY: LIVING, BREATHING GIFTS OF JOY

WHAT YOU'LL NEED:
- Several pads of sticky notes
- A marker for each person

1 Split the pads of sticky notes apart so each person has a handful.
2 Ask participants to write their name on the first sticky note and place it where they're sitting.
3 Have participants walk around the room and write down things they appreciate about the other people in the group (a joyful attitude, a spunky hat, a heart for others, a spirit of encouragement, an infectious laugh,

the way they helped by picking up your kiddos after the last soccer game). Deliver each note to the person's chair.

4 After spending 5-10 minutes writing notes, have participants return to their chairs and read the notes others left. Encourage them to keep the sticky notes in their workbook or Bible to remind them they are fiercely loved.

5 Discuss the following:

- *Which of the notes on your chair surprised you most? Which brought the biggest smile to your face?*

- *Read Ecclesiastes 4:9-16 aloud. In the battles of life, why is it so important to have people fighting alongside you?*

- *What battle are you facing in which you could use some more friends to stand by you, pray for you, and encourage you?*

▶ **PLAY THE SESSION FOUR VIDEO: [22:50]**

Follow along with Margaret and fill in the blanks for each statement below. Take additional notes in the space provided when you hear something that resonates with you.

Tactic 1. ___REJOICE___ when it makes no sense.

Tactic 2. Pray for ___SPRINGS___ ___in___ ___the___ ___dessert___.

Judges 1: 11-15

If the is where I have to live,
  then give me what I need to
survive.

10,000 Reasons by Matt Ludlum

▶ VIDEO DISCUSSION

1 Habakkuk was a man who wrestled with God and embraced Him more deeply. What do you tend to wrestle with God over? When have you grown closer to God by wrestling with Him?

2 According to Habakkuk 3:17-18, under what difficult circumstances does the Old Testament prophet choose to rejoice when it doesn't make sense? Which of the circumstances listed would be most difficult for you? Which have you experienced? Explain.

3 In what square inch are you going to choose to rejoice where it makes no sense this week?

4 Describe a time when God provided springs in the desert for you.

5 In what area of your life do you most need to "get off your donkey" like Aksah and approach your Heavenly Father for what you need in prayer?

♥ CLOSING PRAYER

As you close in prayer ask:

- God to help participants see His handiwork in hard situations;

- God to give each of you extra sensitivity to hear His voice;

- the Lord to renew your hearts with a fresh sense of hope and vision for the future.

Find your square inch + begin rejoicing there.

nab-a-cook
wRestle or embrace

habakkuk 3:17
Phillipians

Jen - Chaa to enroll in school.
Niagra Falls - w/mom
Amy - to find ways to rejoice at work
Kathleen - dating, slow + observant. God to Reveal. discerning
Sandra - diet + exercise motivation.

REJOICE WHEN IT MAKES NO SENSE

 THIS WEEK:

If you're following along in the trade book, read chapters ".007 The Side of Joy No One Talks About," ".008 One Prayer You Don't Pray but Should," and ".009 You've Got to Give This Away," and dive into the five days of homework to prepare for the next gathering.

Caroline bounded into the Corner Bakery with a pink gift bag decorated with cupcakes, chockablock with gifts, and embraced me in a bear hug. From the first moment I met Caroline, I just knew we had to be friends. She radiated joy, sparkled with cheer, and mastered the art of putting the zing in zinger. Somehow this young mom managed to do all this after spending years wrestling with debilitating health issues.

A few years earlier, a high fever and extreme sensitivity to light and sound drove Caroline to the emergency room. The doctor said Caroline needed a spinal tap. He assured her that he'd performed many before. After pushing the needle into her spinal column five times, he had to call in another doctor to complete the procedure.

Caroline recovered from viral meningitis but suffered an epidural headache as a result of leaking spinal fluid. She found that whenever she laid flat on her back, her arms and legs went totally numb.

The spinal fluid continued to leak for the next four years. Doctors attempted to patch the holes. Like a fix-a-flat, some of the fixes took. Others didn't. All needed replacing with time. Caroline, a mother of three children, lived in chronic pain, reduced to laying flat whenever her spinal chord sprung another leak.

 **BONUS ACTIVITY:**

To hear more of Caroline's story, visit *www. carolineholzberger.com.*

"My family and friends would drive me around," she recalls. "I remember laying in the back of Bible study on the couch and just listening. On a good day, I could scoot around the supermarket in one of those specialty motorized carts. Then I would have to rest all afternoon."

Caroline captured that sense of exhaustion in one of her blog entries:

> I'm tired of being in pain.
>
> I haven't had one pain-free day in two years.
>
> I've been flat on my couch 24 hours a day for 11 of the last 16 months.

I'm tired of not knowing what to tell people when they ask, "Well, has it worked?"

I'm tired of seeing perfectly healthy moms seem to take for granted the precious things they get to do with their kiddos.

I'm tired of getting mail from BlueCross BlueShield.

I'm tired of asking God, "What do I have to do to be myself again?"

After sharing her story, Caroline thrust the gift bag into my arms and said, "Open it!"

Inside I found a homemade CD that she had given to all of her friends on the one-year anniversary of having her spinal column glued.

"These were the songs that got me through all those years," Caroline said. "Even when all I could do was lay on the couch, I could still worship God."

Caroline had discovered one of the most powerful tactics when it comes to fighting back with joy:

REJOICE WHEN IT MAKES NO SENSE.

In my health journey, I have been discovering the power of praise. The apostle Paul exhorts us, "Rejoice in the Lord always. Again, I will say rejoice!" (Phil. 4:4, NKJV).[1]

To be honest, when I read this verse, there's something inside me that wants Paul to declare, "Rejoice in the Lord *sometimes*" or "Rejoice in the Lord in the *good times*." Paul challenges us to rejoice in the Lord *always*—meaning in all times, no matter what the situation or circumstance. Paul even writes his letter to the church in Philippi while he is in chains. He rejoices while in prison in Rome.

What is one situation you're facing right now in which it seems impossible to rejoice?

It's difficult to find joy in my struggle with weight loss

Now let me be clear. Paul does not tell us to rejoice *for* all things. We do not rejoice for human atrocities, evil, death, suffering, or pain. Instead, Paul challenges us that even *in the midst* of great hardship we can still find reason to rejoice in the Lord—for His goodness even in the midst of bad circumstances.

 QUOTABLE:

"Joy is the settled assurance that God is in control of all the details of my life, the quiet confidence that ultimately everything is going to be all right, and the determined choice to praise God in all things." —Kay Warren, author and speaker[2]

NOTABLE:

Philippians is considered an epistle of joy with "joy" or "rejoice" used over 16 times.

On the long drives to the hospital for treatment, Leif and I found great comfort in a song by Matt Redman called "10,000 Reasons."

What song has been most meaningful to you during a difficult time?

Why was the song so meaningful?

"10,000 Reasons" is a call to worship the Lord no matter the outcome of the circumstances we're facing. The song's title suggests there are a myriad of reasons to praise the Lord and centers itself in Psalm 103.

Read Psalm 103 and notice the reasons the psalmist gives for praising the Lord. List the five that are most meaningful to you right now.

1   *forgives our sins*
2   *he is compassionate*
3   *everlasting love*
4   *Redeems our life*
5   *slow to anger*

How do you rejoice when it doesn't make any sense?

One square inch at a time.

Leif and I decided to locate those areas where we felt most alone, overcome, depressed, and discouraged, and make an effort to offer God praise in those places. We learned to praise God during the long hospital drives and while sitting in doctor's waiting rooms. I learned that MRI machines and CT scans can even become portals of praise.

EVERY SQUARE INCH PROVIDES AN OPPORTUNITY TO BRING GOD GLORY.

I don't know what your area of pain is right now. Maybe it's found at your desk at work. The classroom where you teach. The empty bedroom in your home. The waiting room at the doctor's office. The assisted living community in which you or someone you love resides. The pillow where you wipe your tears at night.

In that place, you can begin to fight back with joy. You can transform that place of pain into a palace of praise. You can choose to rejoice in the Lord.

Why is this so important?

EVEN THE MOST HUMBLE OFFERINGS OF PRAISE ARE BOLD DECLARATIONS OF TRUSTING GOD NO MATTER WHAT.

Read Acts 16:22-26 out loud. What is surprising about Paul and Silas' response to their difficult situation?

they were praying + singing hymns

What impact does their singing have according to the passage?

It opened the prison doors + freed everyone of their chains

Sometimes when we choose to praise, we feel better. Our spirits lift. Heaviness fades. The spring returns to our step. Other times, there's no immediate payoff and it doesn't seem to make much difference.

Some days I didn't feel anything at all. This may sound strange, but even that was a gift. Praise is not something we do for us, but for Him. The days when I felt nothing were some of the most sincere and meaningful moments of worship I've ever experienced.

On those tough days, we cultivate the practice of joy, choose to worship anyway, and learn to be faithful when it doesn't make sense.

 **CLOSING PRAYER:** Spend time praising God right where you are. Thank God for who He is and His presence in your life. If you feel led, consider singing a worship chorus to Him.

QUOTABLE:

"Far from originating joy, humans are meant to be like an echo, reverberating with God's joy and sending it back to Him. The very word *rejoice* contains (in the prefix 're') this idea of 'over again' or 'back.' The message of joy bears repeating, for in this dark world we need to hear about joy again and again. … True joy is tireless. It's like a little child squealing, 'Do it again, Daddy!' to which our heavenly Daddy replies heartily, 'Yes, let's do it again! And again and again!'"
—Mike Mason, author[4]

BONUS ACTIVITY:

Spend time committing Habakkuk 3:17-18 to memory this week. You'll find a flash card on page 193.

CHOOSE WISELY: DEFINED OR REFINED?

QUOTABLE:

"You don't drown by falling in the water. You drown by staying there." —Unknown

One afternoon shortly after my diagnosis, I was nestled on the couch, tears streaming down my face, when a holy resolve rose up within me. I declared:

GOD WILL USE THIS DIAGNOSIS TO *REFINE* ME, BUT I REFUSE TO ALLOW THIS DISEASE TO *DEFINE* ME.

I had no idea how hard living out that declaration would be during treatment—and still today.

The great adversities of life arrive with labels. The words and phrases used to describe what we've experienced are like prickly burrs—unwanted and tricky to remove. I never wanted to be called "a cancer patient."

Maybe you've had a label placed on you—diabetic, anorexic, depressed, orphan, autistic, always fatigued, sexually assaulted, widow, divorcee, foreigner, single parent, orphan, disowned, home wrecker, unemployed, broke, addict, debtor, overweight, convict, lonely, or elderly.

What is one label that's been thrust on you that you never wanted?

overweight, single mom

Labels can sink deep into our bones. Without even realizing it, we can allow our places of pain to begin defining us. We can become stuck. If left unchecked, we can become victims who live defeated instead of victors through Christ.

Here are 10 signs that you're becoming more of a victim than a victor. Place a check ✓ mark by any of the following that are true in your life.

❏ **I find myself focused on the injustices in my life.**
❏ **I feel like the world owes me.**
❏ **I feel sorry for myself.**
❏ **I keep wondering what I did to deserve this.**
❏ **I feel like people don't appreciate or respect me.**
❏ **I think about how to get revenge on people who have wronged me.**
❏ **I enjoy the attention and validation from others' concern and help.**
☑ **I wrestle with negative thought patterns and inward brooding.**

❏ I sometimes express angry feelings in a way that alienates others.

❏ I use phrases like: "It's not fair," "They should …,"and "They're wrong."

I'm humbled to admit how easily I slipped into the victim mentality. I started to view the events in my life as happening to me. This made me feel powerless, helpless, and overwhelmed.

That's when I discovered comfort in the story of Tamar, a woman who had every reason to unpack her bags in the land of bitterness and disappointment.

Fill out the family tree according to Genesis 38:1-6.

Judah   Shua's daughter

Er   TAMAR   Onan   Shelah

QUOTABLE:

"It may seem a bit strange to put the word 'redeemer' with Tamar, but in Hebrew scriptures the word 'redeemer' means 'to take responsibility for' and refers to persons who take responsibility for others and who call people to responsibility. A redeemer, then, is one who keeps life and love alive, who sees that people do right by each other, who keeps the family going and the community intact."
—Stephen Shoemaker, pastor and author[5]

Tamar lives in an ancient Canaanite culture—one in which women don't have a voice. She is victimized by the death of her husband, her inability to have children, the oppressive customs of the ancient world, a brother-in-law who refuses to fulfill his family obligations, and an irresponsible father-in-law. Tamar has good reason to become a victim, but she refuses.

Fighting back with joy means refusing to give into self-pity, a poor-me attitude, or passivity. Whenever we slip into victim thinking, we feel like we have little-to-no control over our lives and lose sight of God who holds all things together.

How does Tamar fight back with joy according to Genesis 38:15-27?

She took Revenge on Judah by tricking him into getting her pregnant

Tamar's story is one of a redeemer—someone who takes responsibility instead of living as a victim of her circumstances and culture. Judah is willing to give up on the covenant God promised to His people, but Tamar refuses. As a result, she is listed among the lineage of Christ found in Matthew 1:1-16.

Just as Tamar refused to allow the great adversity she endured to define her, we don't have to allow it to define us either.

One day when I was struggling, I sensed the Holy Spirit whisper, "Margaret, you can choose to hold onto the adversity you're facing or you can choose to hold onto God."

I could wrap my arms around the disease and all the nasty effects on my life or I could choose to joyfully wrap my arms around God.

Only one was going to carry me through.

> **Fill in the blank:**
> Today, I can choose to cling to ___*defeat*___
> or I can choose to cling to God.

Joyfully clinging to God isn't a one-and-done decision. We must make it every day. Just this morning I looked at this week's calendar of all the trips to the hospital and let out an "Uggh!" I quickly realized I was feeling sorry for myself, becoming more of a victim than a victor. Rather than give into the sense of feeling powerless, I decided to pray.

Father, thank You that I live in a country with some of the best medical care on the planet. Thank You for the medical team You've given me. Please be with those around the world who don't have such access. You know I don't like medical appointments, but I love divine appointments. Will You go before me? Provide me with opportunities to bring Your joy to others this week. Bless me that I may be a blessing. In Jesus' name. Amen.

With that prayer, I wrapped my arms around God. My attitude soon shifted from dread to divine expectation.

God desires for us to break through the victim mentality. He doesn't want us paralyzed by pain or throwing pity parties. God longs for us to discover that His provision is greater than any problem.

In what way had the man in John 5:1-9 fallen into a victim mentality? How had he allowed his physical condition to define him?

He said he could not get help into the pool. Everyone got there before him.

What does Jesus require of the man to heal him?

Trust in him and get up

In what area of your life is Jesus asking you, "Do you want to get well?"

weight

This story ends with the man going to tell the Jewish leaders that Jesus made him well (see John 5:15). This is important because the man doesn't just acknowledge his condition; he becomes an evangelist and begins telling others about the healing power of Jesus.

One of the key signs that we're busting out of our victim mentality is that we acknowledge and act to meet the needs of others. We begin sharing the good God is doing in our lives with others.

6 TIPS TO BREAK OUT OF THE VICTIM MENTALITY

1 **AVOID THE BLAME GAME.** Be proactive. Take responsibility for yourself and your behavior. You don't get to choose your situation, but you do get to choose your response. What are you doing to seek healing and wholeness?

2 **PAY ATTENTION TO YOUR WORDS.** Notice when you begin whining, blaming, or making excuses. Whenever you find yourself slipping into self-defeating language, return to the passages in Session Three, Day Two: Take Joy Oh My Soul! that remind you of God's unending love for you.

3 **CHOOSE FORGIVENESS.** Whether you've been wronged or committed the wrong, moving forward requires forgiveness. You may not have the strength to forgive yourself and others, but God does. Christ wants to empower you to forgive just as you have been forgiven.

QUOTABLE:

"Do not say, 'I will repay evil'; Wait for the LORD, and He will save you."
—Proverbs 20:22, NASB

NOTABLE:

Type: "Do a barrel roll" into *Google.com*. Squeal in delight when it obeys.

4 **WRESTLE WITH GOD.** After wrestling with a mysterious figure for many hours, Jacob declares, "I will not let you go unless you bless me" (Gen. 32:26, NIV). When you find yourself in the dark and overpowered, wrestle with God until you embrace Him more deeply. Make the same declaration as Jacob, and ask God to reveal Himself in the midst of difficulty.

5 **GROUND YOURSELF IN THE GOSPELS.** Jesus had every reason to become a victim yet He lived as a victor. Spend time reading the story of Jesus' arrest, trial, and crucifixion in the Gospels (see Matt. 26–27; Mark 14–15; Luke 22–23; John 18–19). Take note of Jesus' response to those who wronged Him.

6 **ABOUND IN THANKS.** Remember how blessed your life is compared to people around the globe. Instead of thinking, "I'm the only one," remember the millions around the globe who are suffering. Offer thanks to God for your blessings. Gratitude will change your perspective from what has been taken from you to all God has given you.

What tip would you add to this list?

Take action - do something to move away from being a victim

When are you most likely to slip into victim thinking?

when it gets hard.

What three practical steps will you take to break out of the victim mentality this week?

1 *Get up off the couch*
2 *bypass a snack*
3 *let the braces come*

BONUS ACTIVITY:

Google "Post-Traumatic Growth Syndrome" to learn more about it.

Crisis, hardship, and loss can become opportunities for growth if we respond well.

For years researchers have been exploring Post-Traumatic Stress Syndrome, but more recently they've begun looking at Post-Traumatic Growth Syndrome.

Studies have noted an adaptive growth following trauma that can include a shift in priorities, an increased appreciation for life, more intimate relationships, and a greater sense of strength and possibility. Such appreciable growth doesn't erase or remove the suffering, but allows resilience to grow within the context of personal crisis and trauma. Experiencing such growth requires us to stop being victims.

Describe a time you or someone you know experienced Post-Traumatic Growth Syndrome.

being a single mom made me a better mom.

My prayer is that you will continue to fight back with joy and refuse to give in to helplessness or powerlessness. Remember, our God is mighty to save and longs to heal you. He is with you and for you—even in this. What has happened to you does not have to define you. Instead it can refine you to become more like Jesus.

♥ **CLOSING PRAYER:** Spend some time asking God to reveal any events in your life that have defined you rather than refined you. Ask the Holy Spirit to help you recognize where victim rather than victor thinking pops up in your life over the next week.

💬 QUOTABLE:

"Beloved, we are God's children now, and what we will be has not yet appeared; but we know that when he appears we shall be like him, because we shall see him as he is." —1 John 3:2, ESV

DAY THREE

RECOGNIZE AND REJECT UNTRUTH

Several times a week you'll find me taking early evening walks just to catch up with my sweet friend, Janella. Though she lives in Alabama (yes, she slips a "Roll Tide" into every conversation), we've nurtured our friendship for more than a decade despite the miles that separate us. Over the years, I've watched Janella wrestle with her weight as well as with remaining single. Yet as New Year's Day approached this year something shifted in her life. She decided to do more than try a new diet; she decided to embrace a new way of thinking.

I asked her to share some of her powerful story with you:

> I have always been overweight. It's defined my life. I've been called "fat" since I was in second grade. I've always known I wasn't pretty or popular, and I've always thought weight was the reason. I have felt like less of a person, a failure, a worthless throwaway.

NOTABLE:

Studies show that
thinking positive rather
than negative thoughts
can lead to an increased
life span, lower levels of
depression and distress,
a greater resistance
to the common
cold, reduced risk of
cardiovascular disease,
and better coping
skills during crisis.[7]

When I go shopping with my girlfriends, they browse the "normal" clothes, and I head to the back corner where they keep the "big girl" clothes. We set a time to reconvene. Shopping with girlfriends: together, but alone.

When I hike with friends, they quickly ascend to breathtaking views, but I have no breath left. I huff and puff and find a rock to sit on. They continue without me and find me on the way back down. Spending time with friends: together, but alone.

Describe a time in your life when you found yourself, "together, but alone." *during a small group, believing I was the only one divorced*

I've been told all my life that no guy will ever love me as long as I'm fat. It was not something I ever questioned. "Even good Christian men are still men," I was told; "they want a beautiful girl, too." Whenever I heard that, I would go running to a pan of brownies. Not *a* brownie, but *a pan* of brownies! Food was my frenemy—my friend who consoled me, rewarded me, celebrated with me, and the enemy that held me captive in unending defeat.

Men weren't beating down the doors to date me. In a way, being overweight was a nice, neat reason why I wasn't married. Surely it had nothing to do with me as a person or anything I needed to surrender to the Lord. Surely, it was just because every man wants a beautiful woman.

My struggle with weight has been a lifelong area of defeat. I've been incredibly disciplined and surrendered to the Lord in every area but this. I've been faithful to get up before dawn and spend time in the Word. Faithful to serve on the mission field. Faithful to guard my purity, guard my tongue, guard my heart, guard everything but the temple of the Lord that is my body. It's the one area I've never been able to master. It haunts me as my greatest failure, my greatest defeat, and my cruel captor that holds me in bondage. I've come so close to just giving up all hope and succumbing to defeat.

But in the last year I began to question some of the familiar thoughts and patterns in my mind: No one would love me as long as I'm overweight. God is disappointed in me for what I've done to His temple. I don't deserve to live in joy because I can't succeed in being healthy.

I realized that such destructive thoughts do not come from my Creator.

I mean, fat people get married all the time. I am a child of God; He knows me inside and out and loves me anyway. And really, no one "deserves" to be joyful ... that's the point of grace. It wouldn't be amazing grace if I did something to deserve it.

The truth began to set me free. I made a conscious choice to listen to the truth and banish any untruth. That has made all the difference.

Over the years, I've tried at least nine different diet programs—from calorie counting to diet pills to personal trainers to shakes for every meal. Nothing worked. But in the last 150 days, I've lost more than 50 pounds.

What's different this time?

I am not viewing it as a diet. It's not a behavior change I'm after. It's not even a change in making better choices about what I eat. This is a change in my attitude, heart, and mind. I'm taking Romans 12:2 and putting it into practice. I want to be transformed inside and out. The Scripture doesn't say, "Be transformed by the renewing of your diet." It says, "Be transformed by the renewing of your mind."

I'm looking deeper into not just what I eat but why I eat, which has been interesting and insightful. Difficult, yes. But with every new insight, joy abounds. I'm still in the middle of this tough battle, but the joy from seeing the Lord replace lifelong strongholds multiplies itself and gives me more strength to stand against the fiery darts of the Enemy.

The love of a significant other may or may not come. But a very Significant One loves me exactly as I am. Jesus is the only One who can bring about true and lasting change in our hearts, minds, and bodies. We can use God's truth to joyfully fight for the life we want.

What is most meaningful or encouraging to you from Janella's story?

That she can overcome the hardest things with a mindset change.

In what ways can you most relate to her journey?

this IS my struggle, so I completely relate.

I couldn't be more proud of Janella. The weight she's lost is more than physical— it's emotional and spiritual. Every time I speak to her, she is filled with joy and the love of God splashes through her.

Janella's story reminds us of an important truth:

WHENEVER THERE'S ADVERSITY, THE ADVERSARY COMES OUT TO PLAY.

The Adversary always uses adversity as an opportune time to plant untruths into our hearts.

In one of last week's homework sessions, we talked about the importance of healthy soul talk—speaking God's Word to your soul. Now we're going deeper to detangle the untruths that so easily snare our minds and hearts.

Maybe you've experienced a few of these untruths in your own life. Consider the following:

The parent or spouse who plants a seed of untruth about our worth. We can easily begin believing we're not worth loving.

The diagnosis, health complication, or mental illness plants a seed of untruth about our value. We can begin believing we're not worth keeping around.

The pink slip of unemployment plants a seed of untruth that we don't have anything to offer. We can begin believing God uses other people, not us.

The breakup or rejection plants a seed of untruth that we're not attractive, not fun, not good enough. We can begin believing God tolerates us instead of fiercely loves us.

The rebellious child plants a seed that we're not good parents or we're not cut out for this. We can begin believing we've made a mistake and should give up.

 NOTABLE:

In Matthew 22:36-40, Jesus says the greatest commands are to love God and love your neighbor as yourself. There are three commands of love tucked in this passage: Love God. Love your neighbor. Love yourself. If we don't love ourselves, how are we supposed to love our neighbor well?

Who is the source of untruth according to John 8:42-45?

The devil

Describe his character according to Jesus' words in verse 44.

he has no truth, he is a murderer + a liar

In what situations are you most likely to hear the untruths of the Enemy?

about me physically - you are fat you aren't smart enough

Fighting back with joy requires us to live on high alert for the untruths the Enemy may plant in our minds and be prepared to combat them with the truth of God's Word. The first step is to recognize the untruth the Enemy is prone to whisper in our ears during difficult times.

I recently asked my Facebook friends what untruth the Adversary had whispered in their hearts during times of great adversity. As you read their responses, <u>underline</u> any that you've heard, too:

> "After the loss of my unborn, 'You were never meant to have one.'" —Heather
>
> "You have no usable gifts." —Elizabeth
>
> "The best is in the past. You have nothing to look forward to." —Roxanne
>
> "You're not gonna make it. God will let you down. You don't deserve God's help." —Andrea
>
> "You're a terrible parent and spiritual leader." —Pamela
>
> "You're an awful daughter. You don't really love your mom." —Joanna
>
> "No one will even notice when you're gone." —Rebecca
>
> "You can't be trusted with anything. You're lazy and selfish and always will be." —Marci
>
> "Your story isn't worth telling." —Shelly
>
> "Because of your age it's too late to be pursued, known, loved because it's too late to have babies of your own and a family of your own. Don't even bother to hope. Hope is just a trick. You will live and die alone and unloved." —Michelle
>
> "You were a terrible mother, so that is why I moved your girls away." —Carol
>
> "God's not answering your prayer; He doesn't love you." —Tara
>
> "You're unlovable. The hateful, cruel things that people are saying about you are true." —Melanie
>
> "You have no title in the world, therefore you have no purpose." —Lisa
>
> "God isn't real. Why would a loving God allow your husband to leave you after 30 years of marriage? You are truly alone." —Sandie

Mixed emotions surged through me as I read this list. I tear up because I have heard many of these lies, too. I also become angry because the Enemy doesn't just plant seeds of untruth in our hearts, he does it in the coldest, cruelest ways possible. Reading through these lies should make us even more committed to uproot any seeds of untruth in our lives.

Make a list of five adversities in your life—past or present. Then write what untruth tried to slip into your thinking through the adversity.

ADVERSITY I FACED	UNTRUTH I'M TEMPTED TO BELIEVE
1. being cheated on	I wasn't enough
2. Struggle w/ weight	I am unattractive + unloveable
3. being alone	I'm not a good friend
4. not getting a promotion	you are not good enough at your job
5.	

NOTABLE:

Paul employs militant metaphors in 2 Corinthians 10:4-5 when discussing destructive thoughts that can shield us from the truth of God. In a battle, the winning side is the one who fights under the best general. In our case, we serve the greatest General who can utilize even the most unusual weapons (even joy!) against the Enemy. Paul intends to recapture people from Satan's clutches. Ironically, being a prisoner of Christ is the only way to be set free from being a prisoner of the Adversary.

Crisis, adversity, and hardship provide prime opportunities for the Adversary to whisper untruth into our lives. This untruth disorients us. It distorts our understanding of God, others, and ourselves. Untruth dulls us to the work God wants to do in and through us. The Enemy isn't creative. He just knows our weaknesses and how to manipulate us through false beliefs. Untruth moves us from playing offense alongside God, to playing defense until we find ourselves slumped on the sidelines of life.

Yet even in the midst of great adversity, Jesus wants to reorient us toward Him and His truth.

What does Jesus call us to in John 8:31-32?

Through him we will know the truth + it will set us free

What can purify us from untruth according to John 17:17?

the truth

How can we fight back against untruth according to 2 Corinthians 10:4-5?

the knowledge of God

In the space below, rewrite the five untruths that you're tempted to believe right now (according to what you wrote down earlier in today's homework). Then write a scriptural truth next to it. Use the Scripture passages printed in the margins or find some of your own.

UNTRUTH I'M TEMPTED TO BELIEVE	GOD'S TRUTH
1. I wasn't enough for my husband	I was created by Christ and am a light
2. I am unattractive + unlovable	I am made in the image of Christ
3. I am not a good friend	I am a child of god
4. I am not good enough at my job	
5.	

One of the most powerful ways we can fight back with joy is by grounding ourselves in the truth of God's Word. As Janella discovered:

> The joy in knowing, really knowing, that there is nothing I can do to make God love me more or less is so freeing. Heavy or skinny, God is my Creator, and He loves me. His love gives me so much joy as I see my true value in His eyes. It makes my heart sing and my mouth shut when chocolaty temptation rears its ugly head. Seeing progress in my own attitude and heart produces joy deep within, and that joy fills me better than any empty calorie ever could.

Not only do we need to speak Scripture to our souls, we also need to ground ourselves in the truth of what God says about us and our circumstances. Then we can be set free by the truth of Christ rather than be held captive by the lies of the Adversary and our adversity.

My hope and prayer is that as you fight back with joy, you will recognize any untruth the Enemy has planted in your mind, uproot it, and begin fighting back with joy by clinging to the truth of who you are and whose you are.

CLOSING PRAYER: Spend some time asking God to reveal any untruth that may have slipped into your thinking. Ask Him to show you the truth of who you are and His plans for you through Scripture.

QUOTABLE:

"You are a chosen race, a royal priesthood, a holy nation, a people for his own possession, that you may proclaim the excellencies of him who called you out of darkness into his marvelous light."
—1 Peter 2:9, ESV

"If anyone is in Christ, he is a new creation. The old has passed away; behold, the new has come."
—2 Corinthians 5:17, ESV

"We are his workmanship, created in Christ Jesus for good works, which God prepared beforehand, that we should walk in them."
—Ephesians 2:10, ESV

"There is therefore now no condemnation for those who are in Christ Jesus."
—Romans 8:1, ESV

"To all who did receive him, who believed in his name, he gave the right to become children of God."
— John 1:12, ESV

"You are the light of the world."
—Matthew 5:14, ESV

"In him we have redemption through his blood, the forgiveness of our trespasses, according to the riches of his grace, which he lavished upon us, in all wisdom and insight."
—Ephesians 1:7-8, ESV

RECLAIM WHAT HAS BEEN STOLEN

In the wake of a stock portfolio crashing, a life-altering diagnosis, a layoff, the death of a parent, a separation, a disappearance, life comes to a sudden halt as we try to reassess the new path before us. Trips are cancelled. Celebrations postponed. Plans placed on the back burner. But crisis isn't the only force behind such changes. Sometimes the busyness of life, the over-packed schedules, those everyday stresses eat away at our most precious resources—our time, our energy, our resolve to do the things that bring God and us great joy.

More than a year after my diagnosis, Leif and I were finally able to catch our breath and began assessing the many losses we'd accrued. Much of the previous 14 months felt like a blur as I was forced from procedure to procedure. The moment I healed from one, the next began. The landscape of our lives had been ravished.

That's when I found comfort in the words of the prophet Joel.

Prophetic books like Isaiah and Ezekiel provide a glimpse into the context of prophesy—when, where, why. In the book of Joel, no date or place is offered to set up the scene for the reader. Only a name:

> Joel, the son of Pethuel.
> **JOEL 1:1, NASB**

NOTABLE:

"Has not the food been cut off before our very eyes—joy and gladness from the house of our God?" —Joel 1:16, NIV

One thing is sure, God is the central character of the book of Joel. His intimate name, "Yahweh," occurs 33 times—more than any other word in the prophet's book. Even the author's name means, "Yahweh is God."

Joel darts straight to his point: The entire nation of Judah needs to heed God's warning and join the lament. Certain destruction is coming—one that will be spoken of for generations to come.

This isn't just any destruction, but one that Joel's audience fears most: an agrarian disaster. With everyone dependent on crops for their survival, an infestation of locusts would be catastrophic. Not only will the people have nothing to eat, their animals will starve, too. Joel exhorts the people to rend their hearts back to God.

When God speaks in Joel 2, He doesn't spew wrath. Instead, His words are dashed with mercy and dotted with hope. God's goal is restoration, not destruction.

What happens next? The people are no longer called to weep and mourn, but to rejoice! God, who brought the locust army, will also restore the land. The locusts will eat no longer; God's people will have food to enjoy once again. Joel's audience can't control the storm or swarm, but they can choose to turn to the One who controls all.

Make a list of the restorative promises God makes in Joel 2:21-27.

pastures become green, trees bear fruit, rains, plenty to eat

NOTABLE:

The same words for *locust* are used in Joel 1:4 and Joel 2:25. This provides a repetition of the introduction to the book. The meaning of the words for locust are debated and translated differently throughout Scripture. In every context in the Bible, locusts are associated with overwhelming numbers and greedy devouring.

One of the phrases that caught my attention from this passage was in verse 25 (NIV):

> I will repay you for the years the locusts have eaten—the great locust and the young locust, the other locusts and the locust swarm—my great army that I sent among you.

Perhaps you're an entomologist and well-versed in locusts, but I know little about these insects other than they like to eat their veggies. I decided to turn on the Discovery Channel and do some research.

Locusts are a species of grasshoppers that have entered into a phase where they breed and migrate rapidly. As nymphs (baby locusts), they form bands and crawl around looking for vegetation to devour. As adults, they swarm and search for food. These marching bands and flying swarms are nomadic, stripping fields and destroying crops wherever they travel.

In 1874, a swarm covering 198,000 square miles—nearly twice the size of the state of Colorado—swept through Nebraska. Several organizations monitor this insect, which still inhabits 60 countries around the world.[8]

NOTABLE:

Arbah is the most common word used for locusts in the Old Testament. It's the first word for *locusts* in Joel 2:25 and is also used to describe the locusts that plague Egypt in Exodus 10.

NOTABLE:

In the 1500s, it was common to call someone a "locust" if he or she was greedy.

Locusts can eat their entire body weight in food each day. No wonder they wreak so much havoc and leave such a wide trail of famine, starvation, and poverty in their wake. These devourers deliver destruction.

That's what made the passage in Joel so meaningful. Leif and I felt like so much had been taken from us. We needed God to restore the barren landscape of our lives—to bring us back to spiritual, physical, and emotional health, and in the process infuse us with more of His joy.

We began praying, "Lord, we turn to You to restore our hearts and strength, and we are taking these steps in faith and trust of You."

Leif and I began by making a list of things that were taken from us during the previous year. Here's a glimpse at some items on our list:

What was stolen:

BONUS ACTIVITY:

Locusts are considered kosher by Jewish dietary laws and become a source of food for the poor during famine. John the Baptist is the only biblical character said to have eaten locusts. See Leviticus 11:21-23 and Matthew 3:1-4.

- Enjoying Thanksgiving with the family
- Liking what I saw when I looked in the mirror
- Some of my closest relationships
- Celebrating Sundays at church
- My physical and emotional strength
- Our long-awaited vacation

Then we began to prayerfully consider ways to reclaim those items. I thought of people I missed in my life. I began picking up the phone, reconnecting, and scheduling time together. Because of treatment, I had missed many Sundays at church. I decided to go online and listen to every sermon I had missed. Shortly after the diagnosis, we had to cancel a long-awaited trip to Iceland. This week we rebooked our tickets. Last year I lost Thanksgiving and Christmas to surgeries. This year we've decided to reclaim them with the biggest turkey and most fabulous decorations ever.

I asked my friends on Facebook to share what they are reclaiming in their lives. As you read through their stories, star ✳ any stories that highlight areas you need to reclaim in your life.

"I started college in January. The day I registered for classes I started crying tears of joy. I was taking back the 37 years that the Enemy used to tell me I was not smart enough to go to college. Now I'm a 54-year-old freshman with a 4.0. I may be 80 before I graduate, but I've got a story to tell on my way there." —Linda

"My mother was a victim of Alzheimer's disease. She lived with us during much of the degeneration, and it broke my heart to see the gleam and light disappear from her eyes. In her honor, I make a point to hug the older women who are widows in our church." —Roberta

"It has been four years since my husband and I have ventured away from the house overnight for anything other than hospital stays. We are reclaiming that freedom this weekend. It's just for one night, but we have to start somewhere." —Laurel

"I have not celebrated my birthday in years. This year I turn 40, and I plan to celebrate it." —Jennifer

"My husband and I separated last year. I spent last summer struggling to pay bills and make ends meet. I wanted to do so much with our three boys, but allowed the pain and stress to consume me. This summer we are going on a beach trip and will enjoy play dates at the park. I refuse to spend another minute stressing and living in pain about something that I cannot change. I've given it over to God and have been living in peace ever since." —Jaime

"My father-in-law died 18 days after our wedding. We didn't plan a honeymoon trip in order to spend as much time with him as possible. We've already started saving for a trip to New Zealand. We're reclaiming our honeymoon." — Stephanie

"I've battled with an eating disorder for the past seven years. There hasn't been a day I haven't felt the pull of the Enemy trying to drag me down into a pit of destruction, isolation, and shame. Not until recently did I reach an authentic breaking point and surrender. I now choose to allow my Maker to reclaim my body and use it to write His story." —Alese

"I've reclaimed my Christmas tree. Twice I got a cancer diagnosis at Christmas. So I made a holiday tree and decorated it for two years for Easter, St. Patrick's Day, Fourth of July, and even a Red Sox tree when they were in the finals." —Maura

"I lost both my parents within five months of each other. Three years later, I've reclaimed not feeling ashamed to have fun and smile again. They would be happy for me." —Tara

✚ **BONUS ACTIVITY:**

The act of abundant restoration isn't just something God does, but something He calls people to do. Read Exodus 22:1 and Proverbs 6:30-31.

The joy and delight throughout the responses I received is unmistakable. In each case, her outlook and response is being transformed through the process of reclamation.

In the space below, make a list of things that have been taken from you in the past year. Then add a strategy for how you can reclaim each.

WHAT WAS STOLEN	STRATEGY TO RECLAIM
1. *activities I couldn't do because of weight*	
2.	
3. *cute clothes*	
4. *doing better in my craft biz*	
5.	

➕ **BONUS ACTIVITY:**

What are you reclaiming? I'd love to know how to pray for you. Share your reclaiming story at *www.facebook.com/ margaretfeinberg.*

What encouraging promise is tucked into Isaiah 61:7?

a double portion + inheritance

No matter what has been lost or stolen, God wants to bring restoration to your heart, mind, body, and life—and fill you with great joy. Yesterday has passed, but today is a new day filled with new opportunities and possibilities.

💙 **CLOSING PRAYER:** Spend time prayerfully asking God for His strategies on how to reclaim what the locusts have eaten. Ask the Holy Spirit to reveal the ways in which God has already been at work strengthening and delivering you.

BECOME MORE REAL

As the many months of treatment including surgery and radiation wore on, I began to glimpse a mysterious transformation. The woman I looked at in the mirror was changing before my eyes.

Eyebrows sprung wild and untamed. Eyelashes and nose hairs sprouted again. The toenails that had fallen out started to reappear.

The great adversity had taken a heavy toll on my body. As I stared into the reflective glass, beneath my clothes, I looked like a patchwork quilt. I began counting the scars, then stopped myself at 15 knowing that continuing to count wasn't going to lead to healing.

Around my eyes, dark circles set in and crow's feet deepened. My forehead filled with thick lines; even my gums had receded. In a matter of months, I'd put on 10 years. Staring into the eyes of this new woman, I glimpsed an invisible beauty I'd never seen before, the beauty of becoming real.

QUOTABLE:

"I praise you, for I am fearfully and wonderfully made. Wonderful are your works; my soul knows it very well. My frame was not hidden from you, when I was being made in secret, intricately woven in the depths of the earth. Your eyes saw my unformed substance; in your book were written, every one of them, the days that were formed for me, when as yet there was none of them."
—Psalm 139:14-16, ESV

Mark your responses on the continuum below:

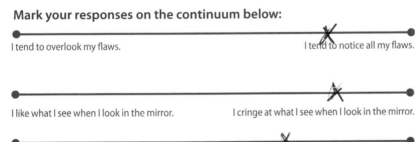

I tend to overlook my flaws. — I tend to notice all my flaws.

I like what I see when I look in the mirror. — I cringe at what I see when I look in the mirror.

I know God loves me just as I am. — I struggle to believe that God loves all of me just as I am.

BONUS ACTIVITY:

Don't forget to continue adding to your Joy Bomb Journal moments in which you've experienced joy from God.

The sight reminded me of Margery Williams' classic, *The Velveteen Rabbit*. First published in 1922, the timeless tale follows the story of a stuffed bunny who arrives in a little boy's life on Christmas morning. As he settles into the nursery, the young bunny becomes insecure when he's tossed aside and begins comparing his cheap velveteen fabric with the more expensive toys.

Have you ever read *The Velveteen Rabbit*? If so, what do you remember about the story?

No

✚ BONUS ACTIVITY:

If you've never read *The Velveteen Rabbit* by Margery Williams, consider picking up a copy and reading it aloud to a child you know.

The wise, old Skin Horse, a character with a prophetic bent, offers assurance and comfort to the rabbit who feels abandoned in the crowded nursery. The Horse predicts the boy will love him, and in the process of being loved a mysterious transformation will occur in which the rabbit will become something called *Real*.

Skin Horse explains that Real isn't how you're made but something that happens to you. It's what occurs when you become your true self—not contrived or pretending, but loved in spite of, and maybe even because of, your imperfections.

Skin Horse explains, "When a child loves you for a long, long time not just to play with, but REALLY loves you, then you become Real."

"Does it hurt?" asked the Rabbit.

"Sometimes," said the Skin Horse, for he was always truthful. "When you are Real you don't mind being hurt."

"Does it happen all at once, like being wound up," he asked, "or bit by bit?"

"It doesn't happen all at once," said the Skin Horse. "You become. It takes a long time. That's why it doesn't often happen to people who break easily, or have sharp edges or who have to be carefully kept. Generally, by the time you are Real, most of your hair has been loved off, and your eyes drop out and you get loose in the joints and very shabby. But these things don't matter at all, because once you are Real you can't be ugly, except to people who don't understand."[9]

More than a heartfelt tale, the parable inspires us to discover our beauty and value on the inside—even when our fur rubs off, extra stitches are required to hold us together, and original parts are missing. Instead of resisting such changes, we can fight back with joy and embrace them. We can learn to hush the self-critical part of ourselves, the nagging voice that reminds us of our flaws, and begin to embrace the possibility that we can be loved just as we are.

Just as becoming real was a painful and arduous process for the rabbit, so it is in our lives. Signs of weakness, dependency on others, and keeping up appearances are the very things that becoming real demands we leave behind.

Through my own journey, I've been discovering that it's not the absence but the presence of wear and tear that awakens us to the depths of God's fierce love for us.

➕ BONUS ACTIVITY:

Watch Colbie Caillat's powerful music video for her song, "Try" on YouTube.

On the continuum, mark how real you feel you've become:

I feel very real.   I wear a variety of masks.

What parts or aspects of yourself do you spend the most time and energy trying to hide?

Feeling incapable at work.
Feeling out of place in familiar
surroundings.

If you really knew me, then you'd know:

I'm self-conscious + not half as
confident as I appear
I fear I don't know enough to be
a valuable employee.

Now stop to think. Among your three closest friends, who knows this about you? Consider sharing what you've written with each of them and your Bible study group the next time you gather.

Something remarkable transpired during my months of treatment. When facades and superficialities were stripped away, my life opened up to more extraordinary people than ever before. People began approaching me and sharing their lives. In the line at the grocery store. At the book table after an event. Waiting at the infusion center. I listened in quiet awe as they stared down life-threatening situations with an ever-renewing hope. Though facing physical weakness and impossible odds, I witnessed those who still demonstrated a defiant joy.

I began to find joy in the privilege of walking and even hobbling among this precious people. Their presence and stories taught me that adversity provides a pathway to becoming more real.

List three situations that have helped you become more real.

1 Leading a team at work
2 Being in small group and admitting my fears
3

QUOTABLE:

"We are his workmanship, created in Christ Jesus for good works, which God prepared beforehand, that we should walk in them."
—Ephesians 2:10, ESV

We can choose to resist. We can cling to our pretenses and facades. We can hide behind shame or religion. We can cloak ourselves in that which is cold and mechanical. We can close the doors of our hearts to others. Or we can open ourselves to the joy of being loved and loving others in our brokenness.

And in the process become more real.

All too often the standards used to determine a person's worth are reduced to increments of beauty, wealth, social status, fame, popularity, or power. Our culture exalts those who conform to particular measurements.

Whenever we give into this thinking, we become like the other toys in *The Velveteen Rabbit*—those who believe that only the shiniest and most modern have value. We begin objectifying ourselves and others until any sense of empathy or compassion evaporates. We soon establish impossible standards. No human can measure up. Joy erodes from our lives.

List three masks you're wearing right now to keep people from seeing the real you.

1 Joking all the time to hide in securities
2 Leading people to hide the same
3

Becoming real strips us of this false thinking and reorients us toward Christ. Through the lenses of Jesus we perceive that every person, no matter what the illness, impairment, or imperfection, is handcrafted *Imago Dei* or in the image of God. Each person is a work of wonder, worthy of honor, respect, and compassion.

All those blemishes and brokenness are gifts meant to draw us together, not split us apart. Each one reminds us of how much we need God and each other. They become points of connection and compassion. Instead of hiding in the shadows, we are freed to enter the light. When you give the gift of being real, you help others see Jesus more clearly and bring comfort and joy.

What does 2 Corinthians 1:3-4 say about how God can use your vulnerability?

God comforts us in our troubles so that we can comfort those who are troubled.

As the months wore on, my weakness leaked everywhere. I looked like the strength mug I described earlier. Broken. Sure, people could see my physical infirmity, but they also glimpsed God's strength and joy on display.

5 TIPS TO BECOMING MORE REAL

1 **EXTEND MORE GRACE, COMPASSION, AND LOVE TO YOURSELF.** The Golden Rule calls us to love others with abandon. But if you aren't gentle and gracious to yourself, then you'll never be kindhearted toward others. Cultivate kindness toward yourself. Ask God on a regular basis how He sees you. Reflect on the Scriptures of God's fierce love for you listed in Session One, Day One: Awaken to God's Fierce Love.

2 **EMBRACE YOUR IMPERFECTIONS.** Like me, you may have parts of your body or personality that you don't like. One way to combat this negative thinking is to stand in front of the mirror and spend time thanking God for how He has made you—even the parts you don't like as much. As you practice embracing your imperfections, you'll find yourself naturally extending more grace to others.

3 **OWN YOUR MISTAKES.** Rather than deny or downplay your errors, be the first to take ownership of your mistakes. Practice laughing at yourself and turning those *oopsy!* moments into funny stories.

4 **TAKE A BREAK FROM WORRYING ABOUT WHAT EVERYONE ELSE THINKS.** All the insecurities and second-guessing what people think makes you do and say things that just aren't true to you. Before you realize what's happened, you're play-acting and pretending to be someone you're not. The next time you're tempted to worry about what so-and-so thinks, pause and ask God for His opinion on the matter.

5 **NOTICE WHEN YOU'RE BEING INAUTHENTIC.** Pay attention to the situations and scenarios that tempt you to be someone you're not. Commit to walk into these places with a stronger resolve to be yourself. Whenever you catch yourself using insincere speech, back up and correct yourself. Not only will the other person appreciate your honesty, but you will respect yourself more.

(Circle) the tip that is most difficult for you. Place a star ✳ next to the one you are going to practice this week.

Let's start practicing being more real right now.

My friends, family, or spouse appreciate me because:

I am loving open + real

➕ BONUS ACTIVITY:

Need a starting point to answer this question? Send a quick text, email, or phone call to your spouse, BFF, or sibling. Ask them to share why they appreciate you.

I appreciate myself because:

*I take charge + get things done
I'm a good mother*

AS PART OF THE BODY OF CHRIST, MORE THAN ANYTHING WE NEED YOU TO BE YOU.

Nothing less. Nothing more. Just the wondrous you God created you to be—real, imperfect, and impeccably loved.

Over the last few weeks, we've covered a lot of ground. We've established joy as our foundation and destiny. We've banished the joy robbers in our lives. We've discovered strategies to fight back with joy.

But what if your situation still hasn't improved? What if you're still facing depression and disappointment, darkness and despair? What if the fight isn't over … it's only just begun?

You aren't going to want to miss the video message for Session Five. We're going to explore the joy that comes with surrender, trust, faith, and hope—even when our circumstances don't change.

♥ **CLOSING PRAYER:** Ask God to remove any masks you may be wearing and help you discover the joy in being who God created you to be.

THE HOLY MESS OF JOY

GROUP GETTING STARTED: (10-15 minutes)

SESSION FIVE:
THE HOLY MESS OF JOY

🗨 HOMEWORK GROUP DISCUSSION

1. Share with the group three moments you recorded in your Joy Bomb Journal on page 168 in which you encountered gifts and joys from God this week.

110 2. From Day One, in what square inch did you choose to rejoice where it made no sense? How did that choice affect you, your attitude, and your outlook?

116 3. In your daily schedule, when are you most likely to slip into the victim mentality? What are you doing to stop being a victim and start being a victor from Day Two?

128 4. From your Day Four homework, what are you feeling most compelled to reclaim?

132 5. What three situations did you list in your Day Five homework that have helped you become more real? How are you learning to become more comfortable in your own skin?

⛓ EXPERIENTIAL ACTIVITY: A BOUQUET OF FAITH

WHAT YOU'LL NEED:

- A flower or two for each person in your group

- A vase (or two) to hold the flowers

1 As group members arrive, hand each person a flower. If you have a smaller group, hand out more than one flower per person.

2 Ask group members to share an area of life in which they're being stretched to trust God. After everyone has shared, ask them to place their flowers in the vase. If you handed out more than one flower per person, you may want to ask them to share an area they're being stretched to trust God for each.

3 Discuss the following:

- *What parallels do you see between the bouquet and what it means to live a life of faith?*

- *What common elements did you notice as members shared where they're being stretched to trust God?*

▶ **PLAY THE SESSION FIVE VIDEO: [21:50]**

Follow along with Margaret and fill in the blanks for each statement below. Take additional notes in the space provided when you hear something that resonates with you.

_____ZeRO_____ is the place where you need God to meet you most.

Joy asks _what_ _if_ _God_.

Joy declares ___But___ ___if___ ___not.___

🗨 VIDEO DISCUSSION

1 What is your "zero"? Where is the place you need God to meet you most today?

2 Which areas of your life are you most likely and least likely to ask, "What if God?" Which leads to greater joy?

3 Ask someone to read Matthew 9:18-26 aloud. After watching the video and rereading this passage, what stands out to you most from the intersection of these two stories? How does each person lay hold of joy?

4 In what area of your life do you need to stop "sizing up the character of God according to your circumstances" and start "sizing up your circumstances according to the character of God"? Explain.

5 Which do you think will equip you to fight life's battles with more joy: "What if God?" or "But if not"? Explain.

❤ CLOSING PRAYER

As you close in prayer ask:

- God to fortify each person's faith in Him;

- that each person's heart, mind, and life awaken to the joy that comes with trusting God;

- the Holy Spirit to illuminate any areas where participants may have been holding back in their prayer lives.

JOY MATURES THROUGH SURRENDER

 THIS WEEK:

If you're following along in the book, read chapters ".010 When Nothing Means Everything," ".011 Life Is Too Short Not to Do This," and ".012 Where I Never Imagined I'd Find Joy" and dive into the five days of homework to prepare for the final session.

My friend Becka and her husband were expecting their third child when, at 37 weeks, their world came to a screeching halt. Becka stopped feeling her baby boy move.

> I'll never forget the doctor saying, "We can't find him," while looking at the ultrasound. Andy was born 24 hours later, not alive, not kicking or screaming, but still. We celebrated him, even if it was only for a few hours. Since then, we try to celebrate him and his short life every day.

Afterward, Becka admits she felt abandoned and forgotten and tossed aside by God. Anger swelled. She begged, "Why?" She couldn't understand why God would have her go through an entire pregnancy to have it end in such sorrow.

> From day one of losing Andy, I knew I was fertile prey for the Enemy to pounce. I made it my cerebral mission to fight. In my heart and emotions, I was so weary; I wanted to give up so many times. But in my head, I knew I had to fight against the Enemy. I would not let him win now.
>
> Honestly, I didn't have much joy that first year. I felt dissatisfied, entitled, and crushed. Fourteen months after our loss, I felt the fogginess of grief start to lift and began to see God as still present; and ever so slowly, I began drawing near to Him. My circumstances were no longer blinding me from the presence of the Lord. I began to feel lighter and happier—like I could breathe a little easier. God filled me with joy.

Becka says she learned personal lessons about surrender through this journey:

> I'll be honest; I'm bossy. I'm in charge. I'm type A. Surrender is not usually my forte. But I did. I had to. I physically could not get out of bed some mornings, which left me surrendering myself to God's people and my community of believers. I had to lean on them and let them help in ways I would not have in the past. I learned I can't do it all, and, therefore, I shouldn't.

> I learned that many people had expectations for my grief and healing. I learned that I had to let those expectations go so that I could root myself in God's expectations of me: to know Him, to know myself, and to walk with Him through the valley of the shadow of death, literally. I did not need to fake being better.

Around Andy's second birthday, Becka read Psalm 139:9-10 (ESV):

> If I take the wings of the morning
> and dwell in the uttermost parts of the sea,
> even there your hand shall lead me,
> and your right hand shall hold me.

For the first time, I believed that God was fighting for me—not on my behalf, not in my stead, but fighting for me to belong on His side. He was fighting for me to come back to Him. And ya know what? He won. He always does.

What do you find most encouraging in Becka's story?

That in the most tragic times, when we can't reach out to God, he reaches us.

What parallels can you draw between Becka's journey and your own?

There are times I've walked away + God pursued me

Becka's story reminds me of what I shared in the video this week. Following God and walking in joy requires us to ask, "What if God?" and declare, "But if not." Coupled together these questions take us to deeper levels of surrender and joy with God.

As we discussed in the video, "What if God?" invites God into the place where we need Him most. Two great examples of this in the Gospels are the story of Jairus and the woman with the issue of blood whose lives intersect when they both seek Jesus (see Matt. 9:18-26).

Instead of focusing on the impossibility of the situation, "What if God?" challenges us to refocus on the possibility of God's kingdom breaking in and transforming us and our circumstances.

JOY ASKS, "WHAT IF GOD?"

What if Jesus wants to bring stillness to the restlessness that's distracting you?

What if God wants to free you from that addiction that's been strangling the life out of you?

What if Christ wants to restore your family?

What if the Holy Spirit wants to move in your church in ways you've only read about in history books?

What if the Lord wants to reveal Himself in your life? Now. Here. Today.

Asking "What if God?" is powerful and awakens our heart and spirit to the work God desires to do in our lives.

What is one area of your life where you haven't asked, "What if God?" What's stopping you?

Most of us know that even if we ask "What if God?," we don't always receive what we want. Sometimes the financial woes increase, the relationship strain worsens, and the health condition deteriorates. That's why:

JOY DECLARES, "BUT IF NOT."

Just as Shadrach, Meshach, and Abednego were willing to face the fiery furnace, no matter what the outcome, we too find ourselves thrust into blazing trials of life. Sometimes God delivers from, sometimes God delivers through, and sometimes God delivers after.

Read Daniel 3 aloud. What is most striking about the resolve of Shadrach, Meshach, and Abednego?

In the space below, list each of the following:

➕ BONUS ACTIVITY:

Spend time committing Romans 5:3-5 to memory this week. You'll find a flash card on page 193.

QUOTABLE:

"Jesus promised His disciples three things —that they would be completely fearless, absurdly happy and in constant trouble."
—G.K. Chesterton, writer and apologist[1]

A specific time God delivered you from a situation:

A specific time God delivered you through a situation:

Through my divorce

A specific time God delivered you after a situation:

What did you discover about God through each of these experiences?

Perhaps the ultimate example of asking "What if God?" and declaring "But if not" is delivered by Jesus on the night of His arrest.

In Luke 22:42, how does Jesus ask, "What if God?"

How does Jesus declare, "But if not"?

As followers of Jesus, we live between the tension of asking, "What if God?" and declaring, "But if not." These two proclamations nudge our minds and hearts, our emotions and spirits into deeper places of surrender. What does it mean to surrender?

SURRENDER IS THE ACT OF YIELDING TO THE POWER OR POSSESSION OF ANOTHER.

When we surrender to God, we yield to Him. But all of us have areas where we're tempted to hold back from God—those subsections of our lives we're hesitant to hand over, those places we haven't asked, "What if God?" and declared, "But if not."

Will you take the next 10 minutes and ask God, "What do I need to surrender to you?"

Sometimes God wants to reveal hidden areas of our hearts to give over to Him. In the space below, begin creating a list of the people, relationships, situations, and concerns that the Holy Spirit reveals for you to yield to God.

Now, take a moment to ask, "What if God?" with each one. Pray that God will heal, restore, renew, rescue, and redeem.

Then, take a moment to declare "But if not." Commit to trust in the goodness and generosity of God in each one—no matter what.

Remember that joy matures as you surrender everything you have and all you are to God.

CLOSING PRAYER: Spend time asking the Father to continue to bring things to mind that you need to surrender to Him.

JOY BECKONS US TO LIVE FOR HIS GLORY

A man recently approached me and shared that he had been asking God for something specific in his life. Despite his sincerity and persistence, God had not granted the request.

"What I don't understand," he admitted. "Is that I've been doing exactly what Jesus commands. I've been praying in Jesus' name. I've been leaning on His promise: 'If you ask Me anything in My name, I will do it.' Yet what I'm asking for remains undone. How do you explain that?"

I recognized the sting of disappointment in his eyes because I'd felt it, too. I suspect we all have prayers we've offered up to God and not received the answer we desired.

At the moment, I'm waiting for God to answer prayers for healing of ongoing pain, a loved one to know Jesus as Lord, and financial provision.

NOTABLE:

Jesus is a form of *Joshua* which means "Yahweh Saves." *Yahweh* or "I AM" is God's personal, intimate name spoken to Moses in Exodus 3. It means the God who was, is, and will be, the eternal, self-sustaining, self-existing, redeeming, promise-keeping God.

What are three prayers you're waiting for God to answer right now?

1

2

3

The man's question compelled me to take a closer look at the passage he referenced from the Gospel of John. On the night of His arrest, Jesus takes time to comfort, encourage, and prepare His disciples for what's coming. Jesus promises:

> "I will do whatever you ask *in my name,* so that the Father may be glorified in the Son. You may ask me for anything *in my name,* and I will do it."
> JOHN 14:13-14, NIV (ITALICS ADDED)

Reflecting on this passage, I thought about all the petitions I had made and heard others pray that were offered, "In Jesus' name."

NOTABLE:

In the Old Testament, a cup often referred to our lives, which can be filled up with salvation or wrath. When Jesus prays in the Garden of Gethsemane, He knows He will drink the full cup of God's wrath—every last drop—as He goes to be crucified for the sins of humanity. Jesus petitions: "Father, if you are willing, take this cup from me; yet not my will, but yours be done" (Luke 22:42, NIV). In the face of certain suffering, Jesus declares, "For Your glory," and drinks of the cup of suffering so we may drink of the cup of salvation.

Check √ the boxes that best describe you:

❑ I never pray in Jesus' name.
❑ I grew up praying in Jesus' name, because everyone did it.
❑ It's my way of trusting my prayers to Jesus.
❑ It's my expression of praying with the power of Jesus.
❑ It's the best way to close a prayer.

What do you really mean when you add the phrase "In Jesus' name" to a prayer?

Sometimes we can slip into adding "In Jesus' name" to a prayer as if it's a shiny gold sticker we put on a petition before God. We secretly hope that if we add this phrase, God will stamp our petition with an "Accept" rather than a "Veto." If we use this secret password, our prayers will be answered in the ways we want.

What's interesting is that you'll never find a prayer that ends with, "In Jesus' name" in the New Testament. Paul offers many prayers throughout his epistles. Consider the following:

QUOTABLE:

"Joy is a mystery because it can happen anywhere, anytime, even under the most unpromising circumstances, even in the midst of suffering, with tears in its eyes. Even nailed to a tree."
—Frederick Buechner, pastor and author[2]

> I pray that out of his glorious riches he may strengthen
> you with power through his Spirit in your inner being,
> so that Christ may dwell in your hearts through faith.
> **EPHESIANS 3:16-17, NIV**

> This is my prayer: that your love may abound more and more
> in knowledge and depth of insight, so that you may be able
> to discern what is best and may be pure and blameless for
> the day of Christ, filled with the fruit of righteousness that
> comes through Jesus Christ—to the glory and praise of God.
> **PHILIPPIANS 1:9-11, NIV**

> Now may the Lord of peace himself give you peace at all
> times and in every way. The Lord be with all of you.
> **2 THESSALONIANS 3:16, NIV**

Paul never adds the phrase "In Jesus' name," which makes me wonder: What was Jesus really getting at when He told us to pray in His name?

I think the answer is found in John 14:13-14 (NIV):

> I will do whatever you ask in my name, so that the Father may be glorified in the Son. You may ask me for anything in my name, and I will do it.

Underline the phrase, "so that the Father may be glorified in the Son."

Do you see it? When we ask something in Jesus' name, what we're really asking is that the Father be glorified.

WHEN WE SAY "IN JESUS' NAME," WHAT WE'RE REALLY SAYING IS "FOR YOUR GLORY"!

Stumbling across this discovery, I started adding "For Your glory" in my petitions to God. I soon noticed significant shifts in my prayer life.

- My prayers weren't as me-centric anymore. They were more focused on God and aligning my heart with His.
- Instead of prayer depending on me, I felt like I was inviting the Spirit to pray on my behalf.
- The outcome of my prayer request wasn't as important. In other words, it wasn't about getting the results I hoped for as much as bringing an increasing amount of glory to God.

No wonder Jesus tells us to pray in His name. When we pray to bring increasing amounts of glory to God, then He will give us what we ask for.

Make a list of five prayer requests you have right now.

1

2

3

4

5

Take a moment to pray for each, adding "For Your glory" to the end.

QUOTABLE:

"It is God who works in you, both to will and to work for his good pleasure." — Philippians 2:13, ESV

John 15:16 (NIV) continues:

> You did not choose me, but I chose you and appointed you so that you might go and bear fruit—fruit that will last—and so that whatever you ask in my name the Father will give you.

Do you see the rich promise? Jesus is saying that when we choose to live lives that are constantly declaring "In Jesus' name" or "For Your glory," we'll find ourselves abiding in Christ. He will do things in and through us that we never thought possible. He will place us on the path to bring Him the most glory in every situation—regardless of the outcome.

I can still see the sting in the man's eyes who asked me why he didn't get what he asked for. Sometimes the things we think are best aren't what God thinks are best. And that's hard. Particularly if you're still unemployed, still single, still wrestling with addiction, still lonely, or still childless. Sometimes on this side of heaven we don't understand why we ask for certain things and God doesn't give them to us. We wrestle with the disappointment.

According to Jeremiah 31:25, what promise does God give to those who are struggling?

Even after we read the promises of God, it can be difficult to lay hold of joy when all we see is the barren land of discontent.

FIVE PRACTICES TO LAY HOLD OF JOY AMIDST DISAPPOINTMENT:

1 **BE HONEST ABOUT YOUR DISAPPOINTMENT WITH GOD.** Tell Him how you feel. Be specific. Let Him know the pain and frustration.

2 **CONFESS THAT YOU ARE LONGING FOR SOMETHING MORE THAN HIM.** Ask Him to forgive you and to heal your heart. Ask God to fortify your faith and enable you to live your life in a way that is wholly and fully glorifying to Him.

3 **REPENT OF ANY FALSE ACCUSATIONS OR BLAMING OF GOD.** Ask God to redeem the disappointment by speaking His love and truth to you.

4 **SEARCH FOR SCRIPTURE THAT SPEAKS OF THE GOODNESS AND GENEROSITY OF GOD AND THE REWARDS OF FOLLOWING HIM.** Commit some of these verses (such as Ephesians 1:7-9, Exodus 34:6-7, and Psalm 65:9-13) to memory. Pray over these passages until you sense God's Word softening and healing your heart.

5 **CONTINUE TO LIFT OTHER REQUESTS TO GOD "FOR HIS GLORY."** Choose to trust Him each day.

List three disappointments you need to share with God.
1

2

3

Now consider the five practices to lay hold of joy. Which of these do you think will be most helpful in you experiencing God's healing and restoration?

Write Psalm 30:11 as a personal prayer in the space below.

QUOTABLE:

"The LORD is my strength and my shield; my heart trusts in him, and he helps me. My heart leaps for joy, and with my song I praise him."
—Psalm 28:7, NIV

God does not want you to be hindered by disappointment. He longs for your life to be marked by joy and trust where each day you bring glory to Him.

CLOSING PRAYER: Spend some time asking God to redeem the disappointments you carry. Ask Him to remind you of His goodness and generosity. End your prayer with "For His glory."

JOY EXPANDS WITH TRUST

QUOTABLE:

"The chance to trust God when trusting isn't easy is wide open, the prospect for modeling hope for a hope-needy world is trending upward. And the possibility of cultivating a storm-proof faith is always going up. This is so because certain truths remain unchanged: God remains sovereign, grace beats sin, prayers get heard, the Bible endures, heaven's mercies spring up new every morning, the cross still testifies to the power of sacrificial love, the tomb is still empty, and the Kingdom that Jesus announced is still expanding without needing to be bailed out by human efforts. God is still in the business of redemption, specializing in bringing something very, very good out of something very, very bad." —John Ortberg, pastor and author[3]

My friend Lizzi was working at the front desk of a dental office when she started noticing something wasn't quite right. Often she'd answer the phone and could barely get the words out. When she did, she slurred or stuttered. She typed throughout the day, but observed that it started taking her longer to peck out a sentence. Sometimes she stared at the keyboard unsure of where the letters were located. Her handwriting began deteriorating to that of a toddler.

She thought it was exhaustion. Drinking more coffee didn't help. A doctor prescribed medicine for vertigo. That didn't make a difference. A friend suggested she visit a neurologist. That's when she discovered she has multiple sclerosis at age 22. MS is a disease in which the nerves of the brain and spinal cord are damaged by your own immune system. The result is a loss of balance, muscle control, vision, and sensation.

Lizzi says the shock of the news left her in a blur. She cried and felt confused about what the future might hold.

> "The only answers I found were that there were none," she says. "MS does what it wants, when it wants. The only comfort I found was that I realized I was wrong. MS doesn't decide what it gets to do, God does. He had a plan, and He still has one. I see glimpses of it every once in a while but for the most part I am still in the dark about what He has going on. There's nothing that I can do about having MS. The only thing I have control over is my attitude toward it."

Despite her physical challenges, Lizzi declares,

> "Jesus Christ is my joy and foundation. People sometimes tell me that I have a good attitude about having MS. I only have one response: What else can I do? God will not let me go. He promises that. My body is temporary, and one day I will have a completely flawless one in its place. God has allowed me to be someone with MS, and so I'm going to be the best one I can be."

Underline the statements in Lizzi's story that are most encouraging to you.

How does Lizzi's story display what it means to fight back with joy?

➕ BONUS ACTIVITY:

In the margin, write Psalm 13:5 in your own words.

One of the most inspiring details of Lizzi's story to me is how she has chosen to display a ruthless trust in God. Perhaps that's why so much joy emanates from her words and heart. She has chosen to trust God in the midst of the storm. She's decided to keep her eyes on Jesus despite the hurricane winds of circumstance, the storm-driven waves of heartache.

Jesus is her joy and foundation.

Sometimes I wonder if it is a similar joy, a desire to trust Jesus no matter what, that compels Peter to step out of the boat (see Matt. 14:29). Peter, along with the rest of the disciples, had spent many months walking, camping, and dining with Jesus. They'd been struck by the power and profundity of His teaching. They'd been awed by the potency of His healing touch.

In fact, they'd just witnessed one of Jesus' most extraordinary miracles. One that's so famous it's the only miracle other than the resurrection that appears in all four Gospels. Jesus takes a handful of rolls and fish, blesses them, breaks them, and then gives them to the multitudes. Thousands feast. Through this marvel, Jesus demonstrates that He is the Bread of life.

Soon after, Jesus sends the crowds away. He instructs the disciples to get in the boat and meet Him on the other side of the lake. Jesus retreats up the side of the mountain to spend time with the Father.

What kinds of gladness, joy, and merriment do the following people experience in Matthew 14:13-21?

The crowds:

they were fed

Jesus:

performed a miracle

The disciples:

Sometime in the evening, a storm blows in. The disciples were likely straining at the oars trying to make headway against the current, wind, and sea spray.

According to Matthew 14:24-31, how is Peter's response different from the rest of the disciples?

Peter put his trust in Jesus but had doubts

Why do you think Peter responds in this way?

because of wordly doubt

Some may say that Peter was a flunkee who took his eyes off Jesus. Or the flop who became distracted by the wind and the waves. But when I look at Peter, I see a man who has taken more steps on water than you or I ever have!

Peter is the disciple who chooses to trust. When he takes that first step out of the boat, he has no idea what his feet might land on. He doesn't know if he will sink beneath the depths or find firm footing. Yet he chooses to trust Jesus regardless.

When distraction gets the best of Peter (and it gets the best of all of us from time to time), the first thing he does is trust again. Peter calls out to Jesus who stretches out His hand and steadies him again.

The Son of God meets Peter on the water and under the water.

Sometimes we're tempted to place our trust in things other than God in the midst of a storm. Circle the ones that are most true for you.

Money	Health	Friends	Family
Parent	Spouse	Determination	Ingenuity
Hard work	Insurance	Grandparents	Job

Circle the facets of God's character that most encourage you to trust Him in the midst of a storm.

All-Powerful	Ever-Present	All-Knowing	Sovereign
Holy	True	Just	Loving
Merciful	Faithful	Wise	Longsuffering
Good	Holy	Foreknowing	Other:

Though Scripture doesn't record this detail, I don't think Peter ever forgot this experience. I imagine years later the disciples reminiscing, "Do you remember that time Pete surfed without a surfboard? Man, that was awesome!" I also imagine Peter remembering this encounter with a big, toothy grin—the joy that comes with having such a sweet memory of Jesus.

Most of us spend much of our lives trying to avoid storms. We're adverse to heavy winds and raging seas. We stay in port waiting for a calm, clear day.

BUT SOMETIMES THE COURSE CHRIST CHARTS FOR US IS STRAIGHT INTO THE STORM.

What connection do you see between joy and trust in Psalm 13:5?

trust unfailing love

Happy is the person who trusts in You, LORD of Hosts!
PSALM 84:12, HCSB

How have you seen your joy increase when you begin to trust God?

I'm lighter, a weight is lifted I'm at peace + able to enjoy more

Sometimes the course includes a difficult diagnosis, an unforeseen financial hardship, or a surprise addition to the family.

Yet that's where He meets us and reveals Himself to us. Joy expands as we choose to trust Him in that place.

♥ **CLOSING PRAYER:** Spend some time praying that God would make Himself present during the storm you are currently facing. Ask that He meet you right here and now.

JOY DEEPENS THROUGH WALKING BY FAITH

➕ BONUS ACTIVITY:

I'd love to hear how God has been revealing Himself to you during this study. Would you be willing to drop me an email at *joy@margaretfeinberg. com?* Your note will make my day!

If you're reading along in the *Fight Back With Joy* book, you know about a hike I took with a handful of friends in Acadia National Park. That's where I first met Nancy. Contagious joy and grace oozed from her. Throughout our weekend together, I learned more about her story and walk of faith:

My husband and I brought our son home from the Philippines a few days before his first birthday. We arrived during a blizzard and quickly introduced him to things like snowsuits and car seats—things he'd never seen in his remote tropical village.

It took a while for him to adjust to us, and us to him, but we learned he was funny and smart, sweet and talented. At age four, after coming home from church, he could sit down at the piano and pick out hymns we'd sung in worship that morning.

My husband and I decided to homeschool our son and his older sister. Homeschooling became a double-edged sword in that, while it allowed me to adapt to and accommodate for my son's learning style, it also kept me from recognizing something was wrong.

During his high school years, as assignments became increasingly. complex, he began shutting down and refusing to do his schoolwork. We assumed we were looking at garden-variety teenage rebellion and laziness. Conventional parenting wisdom suggested we should crack down, remove privileges, and ground him until he stepped up to his responsibilities.

We entered into a season of nearly non-stop battle and confrontation. I was afraid we were losing our son.

In what ways can you relate to Nancy's situation either as a child or a parent?

I had similar struggles with my oldest

One of my husband's employees, who was also an elder at our church and aware of what was going on in our home, asked if we'd ever considered a neuropsychological evaluation for our son. He said our son reminded him very much of a nephew whose life turned around after he'd been evaluated and diagnosed.

We scheduled an appointment and, three months before our son graduated from high school, we learned he had Attention Deficit Disorder (ADD). He had been shutting down not because he didn't want to do his assignments, but because he didn't have the skills and tools to manage the complexities of his high school schedule.

I was devastated, filled with regret and fear. I felt as though what my husband and I had been demanding of our son was the equivalent of asking him to run a race with a broken foot, and then expressing our disappointment when he couldn't do it.

I was afraid we had destroyed our relationship and inflicted emotional wounds on him that he would carry for the rest of his life. We had gotten so many things wrong simply by relying on our own wisdom and assumptions and not asking God to give us eyes to see our son with his unique gifts and challenges.

I have learned there is profound healing power in coming to my child and saying, "I'm so sorry. I didn't know. Will you forgive me?"

It's been four years since our son was diagnosed, and we're still learning about his ADD and how it affects him. We still get a lot of things wrong. Most days, I have no idea what to do or what's best for my son. And I've learned to ask, and keep asking, for help. I thought the responsibility for raising faithful, intelligent, successful, godly children rested so much on me getting things right.

I've learned I need to make time and space in my life for the Spirit to breathe joy and peace into my soul. I've realized the necessity of dwelling in Scripture and allowing His Spirit to knead His life-giving words deep into my heart. And I've learned to lift my eyes to look for evidence of God at work in the beauty of His creation, in the joy of friendships and laughter, music and poetry.

Probably the most important thing I've learned about faith is that everything depends on God's steadfast faithfulness. My faith is a gift from Him, from start to finish, and He's the One at work growing it in me. When I try to put into practice what I consider faithful living, I will inevitably fail in some form or other.

He knows this. And He uses my failures to draw me back to Himself in humility and dependence on Him.

QUOTABLE:

"Though you have not seen him, you love him. Though you do not now see him, you believe in him and rejoice with joy that is inexpressible and filled with glory."
—1 Peter 1:8, ESV

In what ways does Nancy's faithfulness through a difficult situation inspire and encourage you? Be specific.

It's never too late to get help from God. But also we should not rely on ourselves

Nancy's relationship with her son won't ever be perfect, but stepping out in faith allows Nancy to trust God more every step of the way. Sometimes you need to surround yourself with people who fortify your faith in life—and in Scripture.

After a particularly difficult day, I felt a nudge from the Holy Spirit to study the heroes of the faith. I began using Hebrews 11 as a spring board to study the men and women whose names are listed in the roll call of the faithful.

I imagined the joy Abel felt as he gave his first fruits to God. I pictured the delight and holy awe Enoch must have sensed when God met him and took him up. I could almost hear the belly laughter of Abraham and Sarah when they discovered she was pregnant. Through their stories, I began to catch a fresh glimpse of the role faith plays in our lives. Faith is a gift that makes life worth living. Faith calls us to believe in God and to act on that belief. Faith calls us to walk in greater joy.

According to Hebrews 11:1-6, how does faith bring God pleasure or joy?

without faith it is impossible to please God

Why is it important for us to believe God will reward us?

So that we have faith

How does that belief deepen our joy?

Walking by faith doesn't ensure that we will receive all the promises of God on this side of heaven. In fact, Hebrews 11 reminds us that quite often the opposite is true. Yet when we step out in faith, we can do so with the happy certainty that God has something better for us both in this world and the one to come.

After reading Hebrews 11:7-16, what would you say are some of the joys Noah, Abraham, and Sarah experienced by choosing to walk by faith?

📖 NOTABLE:

Barak was a military leader during Deborah's reign as judge over the Jews. His story is found in Judges 4. God commands Barak to gather his 10,000 troops and head to Mount Tabor. Instead of obeying immediately, Barak insists Deborah must go, too. Deborah and Barak follow God's instructions and defeat Sisera's army. Even after doubting God could use him to win this battle, Barak's name ranks with others in the Hebrews Hall of Faith.

💬 QUOTABLE:

"(God's people are those) whose lives are bordered on one side by a memory of God's acts, and the other by hope in God's promises, and who along with whatever else is happening are able to say, at the center, 'We are one happy people.'"
—Eugene Peterson, pastor and author[4]

List two joys you have experienced in your walk of faith.

1

2

✚ BONUS ACTIVITY:

Look up John 16:22. What does Jesus promise in this passage?

Faith is more than just believing that God is able or capable of doing something. Faith calls us to believe in the character of God including His goodness and generosity. The stories of people like Moses, Gideon, and David remind us of the amazing things God can do in and through the lives of those who live by faith.

Make a list of the astounding and joyful acts God accomplished through those who walked by faith according to Hebrews 11:17-35. Place a star ✳ next to those you would most like to experience.

By faith... Abraham offered up Isaac and God provided an alternative.

By faith ... Jacob blessed each of Josephs sons

By faith ... Joseph, spoke about exodus of Israeles

By faith ... Moses parents hid him

By faith ... people passed through the red sea

By faith ...

By faith ...

By faith ...

By faith ...

By faith ...

The author of Hebrews moves from those who triumphed as they walked in faith to those who experienced great tragedy. Yet even amidst the pain and suffering, God was still at work. Those who endured these difficult trials are described as people of whom the world is not worthy (see Heb. 11:38).

Read Hebrews 11:36-40. Mark with an X where you would rank yourself on the continuum below:

●————————————————————————————●

I always choose the easy way out.

I always take the difficult path.

Describe a situation in your life when you chose the easy way out.

diet + quick fixes

Describe a situation in your life when you took the more difficult road.

 **BONUS ACTIVITY:**
Don't forget to continue adding moments you've experienced joy from God to your Joy Bomb Journal.

As I spent time digging deeper into each of the lives of those mentioned in Hebrews 11, I began to recognize a common thread:

THE JOURNEY OF FAITH WILL ALWAYS TAKE US TO PLACES WHERE WE NEED GOD MORE.

Though we may not be called by God to build a cruise ship or spend four decades hiking through the desert, the life of faith always leads to impossible situations—places where we find ourselves crying out, "Only God!"

Only God can save. Only God can heal. Only God can redeem. Only God can work something good out of this. Only God.

What Only God! situation are you facing right now? Describe.

weight loss

QUOTABLE:

"The hope of the righteous brings joy."
—Proverbs 10:28, ESV

If you find yourself in an Only God! situation, draw comfort from Hebrews 11. You are not alone. Though the life of faith always leads to great joy, it is often marked by great pain. The difficulties you're facing may be confusing. Perhaps you didn't expect the Christian life to turn out like this. Maybe the challenges you're enduring are heartbreaking. Or, like mine, they're life shattering.

Even in the middle of what you're facing, God is still at work. He hasn't left you. You must remember that the trials you're facing are only temporary. You will ultimately experience the joy of what only God can do with your life. Now, more than ever, is the time to fix your eyes on Jesus the Author and Perfecter of your faith. Stand firm. Remain faithful.

As we close this lesson, can I pray for you?

Heavenly Father, You know the Only God! situation my sweet friend is facing. I ask that You make Your presence known in the midst. Wrap him or her in Your loving arms, fill my friend with Your joy. Whisper Your love today. Remind my friend that he or she is a beloved child of the King. For God's glory. Amen.

❤️ **CLOSING PRAYER:** Spend time prayerfully considering how God is calling you to step out in faith to follow Him into uncharted territory.

JOY ABOUNDS IN HOPE

One of my dearest friends on the planet, Carol, is one of the most delightful, warm, loving people you'll ever meet. But you'd never expect that she grew up without parents. At the age of five, she found her mother dead. Because her father was incapable of caring for her and her two siblings, she was forced to grow up in a children's home. Carol remembers that everyone at the orphanage shared a common bond: family abandonment, dysfunction, and horror stories.

"The public school we attended had kids who didn't wear their trials on their sleeves like us," she recalls. "We were easy marks for being made fun of and shunned. Many of the kids were looked on with pity instead of hope. Expectations for success were low. I remember telling someone I would go to college. They said, 'What makes you think you can do that?'"

Yet Carol says that despite the hardships of her childhood, she kept seeing the fingerprints of God in her life. "No matter how far I ran from Him, He placed people in my life to help me grow spiritually and form my own family," she says. "One day, God whispered 'You are mine. Don't listen to those who say you can't.' He made me realize that even though others wouldn't claim me, I was His daughter. I've held onto hope in Him, and He has blessed me beyond my wildest dreams."

Carol didn't just end up attending a university, but today she runs her own department at a college. She's always keeping an eye out for students who experienced difficult childhoods and goes out of her way to impart to them the hope she received through Christ.

Carol reminds me that hope is oxygen for the believer who is short of breath. Hope is the life preserver we cling to when everything says to let go. The odds

QUOTABLE:

"Hope can get sick and die. Sometimes hope is murdered with shocking quickness when the one thing on which we set our deepest hope is blown out of our lives, like a tent in the path of a hurricane. Other times hope dies slowly, sliced away in bits and pieces of disappointment; one thing after another that we had hoped for whittled away, like wood chips flying from a green branch before the knife of an indifferent whittler. Whether it slips slowly like drippings from a leaking valve or gets smashed on the rocks of reality, when hope dies inside of us, we are all but done for." —Lewis Smedes, author and professor[5]

may be long, the statistics against us. But hope doesn't pay attention to the numbers. All hope needs to thrive is the belief that what we hope for is possible through Jesus Christ.

On the meter below, fill in how hopeful you are right now.

EMPTY		⟍				FULL

Hopeless   **Abounding in hope**

Hope is what followers of Jesus have been called to cling to for thousands of years. This becomes extra challenging considering the world we live in is fumigated with the stench of sin and death. You don't have to skip a rock far to hit needless suffering and injustice. Sometimes the pain we witness can make us second-guess God and lose hope.

Fill in the chart below. What situations are you facing right now that tempt you to think the following?

QUOTABLE:

"The disciples were filled with joy and with the Holy Spirit."
—Acts 13:52, ESV

STATEMENT	SITUATION
God isn't really good.	
God really can't heal.	
God isn't anywhere to be found in this situation.	
God won't really forgive me; my sin is too big.	
God can't reach this person I've been praying for all these years.	

Though we and the people we love face seemingly impossible situations, God continues to ask us to place our hope in Him. And when we do, we will find that our hope is in a Person and the promises He makes.

One of the bedrock passages on hope is found at the beginning of Romans 5. It's written by Paul, a man whose life and ministry clenched tight to the hope found in Christ.

On far too many nights, Paul languishes in a dark prison cell, dog paddles among driftwood from a shipwreck, and nurses the wounds of yet another public beating. During the midnight hours, he wonders if it was all worth it. Doubt whispers that the Jesus he met on the roadside was a hallucination or a figment of his imagination. Temptation beckons him to walk. Despair sighs he should turn away once and for all.

Yet Paul remains undeterred and exudes the joy that accompanies living with dynamic faith. This is the man who commands us to:

> Rejoice in hope.
> ROMANS 12:12, ESV

Indeed, joy and hope walk hand in hand.

Have you met someone who is joyful but hopeless?

No

What about hopeful but joyless?

No

What connection have you experienced between hope and joy?

Those that have joy usually have hope + vice versa

This isn't just prescriptive for Paul. Somewhere along the way, he's discovered a connection between hope and joy that he doesn't want us to miss. Interwoven throughout the book of Romans are powerful reminders that no matter the circumstances we find ourselves in, we are called to walk in an unmistakable happy certainty with God.

Paul writes:

> Therefore, since we have been justified by faith, we have peace with God through our Lord Jesus Christ. Through him we have also obtained access by faith into this grace in which we stand, and we *rejoice* in hope of the glory of God.
> ROMANS 5:1-2, ESV (ITALICS ADDED)

The apostle reawakens us to the depths of what Jesus Christ has done for us. The Only Child of God crashed into our world as an infant born among farm animals to deliver the best news our planet ever received. Through His blistering death and jaw-dropping resurrection, we are extended an invitation to live with God, without hindrance, forever.

NOTABLE:

Happy certainty: A joyful, hope-filled, unshakable confidence in God.

QUOTABLE:

"Hope, for the Christian, is not wishful thinking or mere blind optimism. It is a mode of knowing, a mode within which new things are possible, options are not shut down, and new creation can happen." —N.T. Wright, theologian[6]

JESUS CAME HOPE-*FILLED* TO MAKE US HOPE*FUL*.

This is no passive gift, a trinket to tuck away in a cluttered kitchen drawer.

As we embrace and embody all Jesus has done for us and wants to give us, we find ourselves adorned in grace, overflowing with joy, and radiant with hope.

Paul continues:

> Not only so, but we also glory in our sufferings, because we know that suffering produces perseverance; perseverance, character; and character, hope.
> **ROMANS 5:3-4, NIV**

Did you see the curve ball Paul just threw? In Romans 5:1-2, Paul rejoices in hope. In Romans 5:2-3, Paul rejoices in suffering.

Reflecting on Romans 5:1-5, how does Paul find joy in both hope and suffering?

even in suffering you need hope... more so

What would it look like for you to discover joy in hope in your situation?

these are kind of the same

What would it look like for you to discover joy in suffering in your situation?

hope will make whatever situation your in, easier

Paul's thinking looks something like this:

TROUBLE PRODUCES PATIENCE. PATIENCE PRODUCES CHARACTER. CHARACTER PRODUCES HOPE. HOPE PRODUCES ANOTHER REASON TO REJOICE.

In the space below, put Paul's encouraging words in the correct order: hope, suffering, perseverance, glory, character.

Suffering, character, hope, perseverance, glory

No matter what the situation, we can discover happy certainty in God by recognizing that even in the toughest of times God is doing something in and through us. Patience is budding within us. Our character is looking more like Christ. Our hearts are being filled with a heavenly hope.

What situation are you facing right now that's forcing you to become more patient? That's forging your character? That's driving you to cling to the hope that can only be found in Christ?

Even in this, you can begin to walk with the happy certainty that comes with knowing God is with you and for you.

Paul unearthed the joy that comes with hope. And we can, too.

My friend, Kay, struggled with hope after her son, Matthew, took his life. She began asking God to start rebuilding her hope for what was next in her life. As she stumbled on verses, she began placing them in a hope box. The container soon filled with passages like 1 Corinthians 15:43 (NLT) which says:

> Our bodies are buried in brokenness, but they will be raised in glory. They are buried in weakness, but they will be raised in strength.

As a result, hope is alive in her again.[8]

You're not going to want to miss the final party. Oops! I mean gathering. Now that we've learned how to fight back with joy, we are going to help others fight back with joy. Don't forget to bring gift cards, note cards, and a list of people you can encourage who have been facing challenging circumstances. This powerful final session is all about the joy of the kingdom of God breaking into other people's lives as we fight back with joy together.

✚ BONUS ACTIVITY:

You may want to start your own hope box. Ask God to give you passages that don't just breathe hope into you again, but also joy.

❤ **CLOSING PRAYER** Spend time asking God to renew your hope in Him and anchor you in His joy no matter what circumstance you are facing. Fix your eyes on Him.

WHAT TO DO WHEN THOSE YOU LOVE ARE HURTING

GROUP GETTING STARTED: (10-15 minutes)

SESSION SIX:
WHAT TO DO WHEN THOSE YOU LOVE ARE HURTING

NOTE: UNLIKE OTHER LESSONS, THE EXPERIENTIAL ACTIVITY IS DESIGNED TO COME AFTER THE VIDEO. PLEASE PREVIEW IN ADVANCE WHAT YOU'LL NEED FOR THE WEEK.

HOMEWORK GROUP DISCUSSION

1. Share with the group three moments you recorded in your Joy Bomb Journal on page 168 in which you encountered gifts and joys from God this week.

2. Recall Becka's story in your homework from Day One. What was most meaningful or encouraging to you? What do you relate to most from her story and the lesson on surrender?

Pg 141

3. From Day Three, when you're in the middle of a storm, where are you tempted to place your trust other than God?

152

4. In what situations are you tempted to choose temporary pleasure over the more difficult path God has for you from Day Four?

158

5. Based on Day Five homework, how have you discovered joy and clung to hope in the midst of adversity?

6. On a scale of 1 to 10, how would you rate your level of joy today? Circle the number.

1   2   3   4   5   6   ⑦   8   9   10

Now turn to page 15 and compare your answer today with your answer from Session One, Day One. How has your joy level changed? What actions or circumstances have led to that change over the last five sessions?

▶ **PLAY THE SESSION SIX VIDEO: [27:25]**

Follow along with Margaret and fill in the blanks for each statement below. Take additional notes in the space provided when you hear something that resonates with you.

Tactic 1. Give the gift of ___*your*___ ___*presence*___.

Tactic 2. Be slow to ___*speak*___.
listening, being present

Today, you're in my thoughts, you're in my prayers, and you are ___*loved*___.

Tactic 3. Think ___*long-term*___.
Set a reminder to send something (a call, a card, a text) every 2-4 weeks

Tactic 4. Be ___*practical*___.
ask! Everyone's needs are different.

Tactic 5. Ask God how to ___*pray*___.
Luke 11   *Be a Joy Bomber!*

▣ **VIDEO DISCUSSION**

1 During your times of loss, pain, or crisis, what have been the most helpful things people have said or done? What were the most hurtful or unhelpful?
2 Reflecting on the difficult time of a loved one, how do you wish you would have responded differently?
3 What reasoning do you use that results in you not giving the gift of your presence to those who are facing hard times?
4 Who are five people you need to break the silence with today?

Renée
Madison

◀ EXPERIENTIAL ACTIVITY: BREAKING THE SILENCE

WHAT YOU'LL NEED:

- Each participant to bring a snack to share as well as a gift card to a gas station, grocery store, movie theater, etc. that can be given to someone who is going through a tough time
- A few boxes of notecards or stationery and envelopes
- Stamps
- Fun background music
- Party balloons and fun decorations
- A pen and sheet of paper for each person

1 Decorate the room with balloons, streamers, wildflowers, and anything you can find to create a joyous, celebratory atmosphere.
2 Invite participants to make a list of people in their lives who are going through a difficult time. Encourage them to go through their cell phone contacts for people they may have forgotten as well as to get people's addresses.
3 Hand out notecards or stationery. Ask participants to handwrite notes of encouragement letting those going through challenging times know they are remembered, prayed for, and loved. Include gift cards when available and appropriate.
4 Enjoy laughing, talking, sharing, and catching up as you eat together.
5 Before you close, invite participants to fill out the I Will #FightBackWithJoy By … on page 183. Take pictures of the group holding up the page and send us your photo at *joy@margaretfeinberg.com*. We'd love to post your pictures on our website.

♥ CLOSING PRAYER

As you close in prayer ask:

- God to continue expanding each person's spectrum of joy;
- God to continue revealing fresh strategies in each person's life for how to fight back with joy;
- the Holy Spirit to continue creating opportunities to grow closer to Him and each other.

JOY BOMB JOURNAL

One of the ways we know God is here is that He tosses joy bombs at us all day, every day. Sometimes God fills the balloon of joy with helium to refocus our gaze above. Other times He fills it with water. It becomes like those soft, cool water balloons that broke over us as kids on a 100 degree day. James 1:17 (ESV) says that God is behind "every good and perfect gift."

What are the joy bombs God is tossing at you? What are those moments where God is illuminating your night sky? Those places where you hear an unexpected pop and turn to see a sizzling, sparkling bouquet above? Who are the people God has dropped in your life who have exploded your depression, obliterated your cynicism, blown up your tendencies to see the world as a glass half-full? That sympathetic coworker, that always available friend, that arm around your slumping shoulder. What joy bomb is God tossing at you today?

I'd like you to begin keeping track of the joy bombs in your life by recording three of them each day. Since there are 25 days of homework in this study, we've left room for you to write down 75 joy bombs. Place a check mark next to each day after you record the gifts God is giving you.

☒ *EXAMPLE DAY: DATE:* May 7, 2015

- Snuggles from Hershey the Superpup

- A beautiful sunset

- An unexpected phone call from a dear friend

☑ *DAY 1: DATE* June 9, 2015

- Seeing my son Madison step up to help without being asked

- having my difficult conversation with a co-worker go well

- Hunter, telling me he loves me today even in a joking manner.

☐ *DAY 2: DATE*

-
-
-

☐ *DAY 3: DATE*

-
-
-

☐ *DAY 4: DATE*

-
-
-

☐ *DAY 5: DATE*

-
-
-

☐ *DAY 6: DATE* June 21, 2015

- Celebrating father's day w/ Mike quality time w/ the boys

- Madison opening up about the pain he's suffering

-

☐ *DAY 7: DATE*

- Finishing up the iteration with less stress than last time

-

-

☐ *DAY 8: DATE* Thurs 25th

- Dinner with Amy

- Hockey Game with co-workers + taking my boys along.

-

☐ *DAY 9: DATE* Saturday

- Napping on a rainy day

- Make picking up breakfast

- Date Night with great food and funny movie

☐ *DAY 10: DATE* Sunday June 28th

· Leisurely food shopping + Michaels

· Good message heard for first time by youth pastor

·

☐ *DAY 11: DATE*

· See a photos from Father's Day that made me smile

· Warm soup after a cold day in the office.

·

☐ DAY 12: DATE

- seeing chase in photos on facebook

- Hunters pride at his success on a cull

-

☐ DAY 13: DATE

- had a long chat with madisen on his birthday

- Received another letter from Chase

- Survived a bike ride

☐ DAY 14: DATE

-
-
-

☐ DAY 15: DATE

-
-
-

□ *DAY 16: DATE*

-
-
-

□ *DAY 17: DATE*

-
-
-

☐ *DAY 18: DATE*

-
-
-

☐ *DAY 19: DATE*

-
-
-

☐ DAY 20: DATE

- _____
- _____
- _____

☐ DAY 21: DATE

- _____
- _____
- _____

☐ *DAY 22: DATE*

-

-

-

☐ *DAY 23: DATE*

-

-

-

☐ *DAY 24: DATE*

-
-
-

☐ *DAY 25: DATE*

-
-
-

I WILL #FIGHTBACKWITHJOY BY ...

What tactics are you going to use to fight back with joy? Will you embrace celebration as a discipline? March forth with mirth? Rejoice when it makes no sense? Follow the directions below and join others around the world in a photo collection that describes the ways we will use joy as a weapon. Here's how:

FIRST ...

• Write down your answer to "I will #fightbackwithjoy by ..." on the following page. Or download more copies at *fightbackwithjoy.com*.

NEXT ...

• Take a photo of yourself with your sign.

FINALLY ...

• Email your photo to *joy@margaretfeinberg.com*.

• Share your photo on Margaret Feinberg's Facebook wall.

• Tweet and Instagram your photo using #fightbackwithjoy.

• Hang your answer around your house or workplace as a daily reminder to fight back with joy.

TIPS AND HINTS ...

• There's no right or wrong answer. Feel free to use one of the tactics from the weekly homework.

• Use a large, dark marker for readability.

• Be creative. Photos will be featured on Margaret's website, Facebook, and/or Twitter.

I WILL #FIGHTBACKWITHJOY BY...

ENDNOTES

DEAR GROUP MEMBER

1. Scripture quotations marked HCSB are taken from the Holman Christian Standard Bible®, Copyright © 1999, 2000, 2002, 2003, 2009 by Holman Bible Publishers. Used by permission. Holman Christian Standard Bible®, Holman CSB®, and HCSB® are federally registered trademarks of Holman Bible Publishers.

SESSION 1

1. All Scripture marked NIV are taken from the Holy Bible, NEW INTERNATIONAL VERSION®. Copyright © 1973, 1978, 1984, 2011 by Biblica, Inc. All rights reserved worldwide. Used by permission.
2. All Scripture marked MSG are taken from The Message. Copyright © 1993, 1994, 1995, 1996, 2000, 2001, 2002. Used by permission of NavPress Publishing Group.
3. Scripture quotations marked GNT are from the Good News Translation in Today's English Version—Second Edition Copyright © 1992 by American Bible Society. Used by permission.
4. Scripture marked NCV is from the New Century Version®. Copyright © 1987, 1988, 1991 by Thomas Nelson, Inc. Used by permission. All rights reserved.
5. Scripture quotations marked NLT are taken from the Holy Bible, New Living Translation, copyright © 1996. Used by permission of Tyndale House Publishers, Inc., Wheaton, IL 60189 USA. All rights reserved.
6. Thomas Aquinas, *Summa Theologica* (la.xe i.3, ad 3). Available from the Internet: *archive.org/stream/stthomasaquinasp029194mbp/*.
7. Scripture quotations marked KJV are taken from the Holy Bible, King James Version.
8. Scripture quotations marked NASB are taken from the New American Standard Bible®, Copyright ©1960, 1962, 1963, 1968, 1971, 1972, 1973, 1975, 1977, 1995 by The Lockman Foundation. Used by permission. (*www.lockman.org*)
9. Jonathan Edwards, "Discourse on the Trinity," *Writings on the Trinity, Grace, and Faith*, ed. Harry S. Stout (New Haven, CT: Yale University Press, 2003), 27.
10. Greg Forster, *Joy for the World: How Christianity Lost Its Cultural Influence and How It Can Begin Rebuilding It* (Wheaton, IL: Crossway, 2014), 34.
11. Matthew Elliott, *Feel: The Power of Listening to Your Heart* (Carol Stream: Tyndale, 2008), 174.
12. Henri Nouwen, as quoted by Angela Thomas, *Choosing Joy* (New York: Howard Books, 2011), 67.
13. Scripture quotations marked ESV are from The Holy Bible, English Standard Version® (ESV®), copyright © 2001 by Crossway, a publishing ministry of Good News Publishers. Used by permission. All rights reserved.
14. William P. Brown, as quoted by Terence E. Fretheim, "God Creation and the Pursuit of Happiness," *The Bible and the Pursuit of Happiness: What the Old and New Testaments Teach Us about the Good Life,* ed. by Brent A. Strewn (New York: Oxford University Press, 2012), 41.
15. Nancy Rothbard, "Put on a Happy Face. Seriously.,"*The Wall Street Journal*

(online), 24 October 2011 [cited 27 October 2014]. Available from the Internet: *online.wsj.com.*

16. *Star Trek II: The Wrath of Khan,* directed by Nicholas Meyer (1982, Los Angeles, CA: Paramount Studios).

17. Elizabeth W. Dunn and Michael Norton, "Hello, Stranger," *New York Times* (online), 25 April 2014 [cited 27 October 2014]. Available from the Internet: *www.nytimes.com.*

SESSION 2

1. Lou Dzierzak, "Factoring Fear: What Scares Us and Why," *Scientific American* (online), 27 October 2008 [cited 3 October 2014]. Available from the Internet: *www.scientificamerican.com.*

2. "Chemistry of Fear," *Huffington Post* (online), 29 Oct. 2013 [cited 3 October 2014]. Available from the Internet: *www.huffingtonpost.com.*

3. Susan Johnston, "5 Bankruptcy Myths Debunked," *U.S. News* (online), 14 May 2012 [cited 3 October 2014]. Available from the Internet: *money.usnews.com.*

4. "Breast Cancer Risk in American Women," *National Cancer Institute* (online), 24 September 2012 [cited 3 October 2014]. Available from the Internet: *www. cancer.gov.*

5. "Prostate Cancer Overview," *American Cancer Society* (online), 12 September 2014 [cited 3 October 2014]. Available from the Internet: *www.cancer.org.*

6. "Marriage and Divorce," *American Psychological Association* (online), [cited 3 October 2014]. Available from the Internet: *www.apa.org/topics/divorce.*

7. "Alzheimer's Facts and Figures," *Alzheimer's Association* (online), [cited 3 October 2014]. Available from the Internet: *www.alz.org.*

8. Frederick Buechner, "Clown in the Belfry," *FrederickBuechner.com* (online), [cited 3 October 2014]. Available from the Internet: *www.frederickbuechner.com/ content/clown-belfry-page-175.*

9. Angela Thomas, *Choosing Joy* (New York: Howard, 2011), 4.

10. "Tired & Stressed, but Satisfied," *Barna Group* (online), 6 May 2014 [cited 3 October 2014]. Available from the Internet: *www.barna.org.*

11. Leonard Sweet, *The Well-Played Life* (Carol Stream, IL: Tyndale, 2014), 11.

12. Michael J. Breus, "Too Little Sleep and Weight Gain? It's a Brain Thing," *Huffington Post* (online), 1 September 2013 [cited 3 October 2014]. Available from the Internet: *www.huffingtonpost.com.*

13. Annalyn Kurtz, "World's shortest work weeks," *CNN* (online), 10 July 2013 [cited 3 October 2014]. Available from the Internet: *money.cnn.com.*

14. Katia Hetter, "Get happy in the world's happiest countries," *CNN* (online), 21 March 2014 [cited 3 October 2014]. Available from the Internet: www.cnn.com.

15. Katie Johnson, "For majority of workers, vacation days go unused," *Boston Globe* (online), 30 December 2013 [3 October 2014]. Available from the Internet: *www.bostonglobe.com.*

16. Nathan MacDonald, "Is there Happiness in the Torah?," *The Bible and the Pursuit of Happiness: What the Old and New Testaments Teach Us about the Good Life,* Brent A. Strewn, ed. (New York: Oxford University Press, 2012), 73.

17. Gary Thomas, "All Work and No Play …," *Relevant Magazine* (online), 3 August 2010 [cited 3 October 2014]. Available from the Internet: *www.relevantmagazine.com.*

SESSION 3

1. Oswald Chambers, as quoted by Ray Johnston, *The Hope Quotient* (Nashville: W Publishing, 2014), 71.
2. Patsy Clairmont, *Twirl: A Fresh Spin at Life* (Nashville: Thomas Nelson, 2014), 23-24.
3. N.D. Wilson, "Lighten Up, Christians: God Loves a Good Time," *Christianity Today* (online), 7 May 2014 [3 October 2014]. Available from the Internet: *www.christianitytoday.com*
4. A. W. Tozer, as quoted by Matthew Elliott, *Feel: The Power of Listening to Your Heart* (Carol Stream, IL: Tyndale House Publishers, 2008), 4.
5. Rabbi Debra Orenstein, "The Jewish Rites of Death and Mourning," RabbiDebra.com (online), 2008 [cited 3 October 2014]. Available from the Internet: *www.rabbidebra.com/support-files/ritesofdeath.pdf*.
6. Gerald L. Stittser, *A Grace Disguised: How the Soul Grows through Loss* (Grand Rapids: Zondervan, 1995), 63.
7. R. R. Melick. *Philippians, Colossians, Philemon* (Nashville: Broadman & Holman Publishers, 1991).

SESSION 4

1. Scriptures marked NKJV are from the New King James Version. Copyright © 1979, 1980, 1982, Thomas Nelson, Inc., Publishers.
2. Kay Warren, *Choose Joy: Because Happiness isn't Enough* (Grand Rapids: Revell, 2012), 32.
3. Jerry Bridges, *The Practice of Godliness* (Colorado Springs: NavPress, 1996), 115.
4. Mike Mason, *Champagne for the Soul* (Colorado Springs: Waterbrook, 2003), 8.
5. Stephen Shoemaker, *GodStories: New Narratives from Sacred Texts* (Valley Forge: Judson Press, 1998), 75.
6. Jerry M. Lewis, "Posttraumatic Growth Syndrome: Fact or Fiction," *Psychiatric Times* (online), 1 December 2007 [cited 6 October 2014]. Available from the Internet: *www.psychiatrictimes.com*.
7. "Positive thinking: Stop negative self-talk to reduce stress," *Mayo Clinic* (online), 4 May 2014 [cited 6 October 2014]. Available from the Internet: *www.mayoclinic.org*.
8. Matthew Garcia, "Melanoplus spretus: Rocky Mountain Locust," *Animal Diversity Web* (online), 2000 [cited 6 October 2014]. Available from the Internet: *animaldiversity.ummz.umich.edu*.
9. Margery Williams, *The Velveteen Rabbit or, How Toys Become Real* (Philadelphia: Running Press, 1998), 14-16.

SESSION 5

1. G.K. Chesterton, as quoted by Ray Johnston, *The Hope Quotient* (Nashville, TN: W Publishing, 2014), 185.
2. Frederick Buechner, "Touched with Joy," *FrederickBuechner.com* (online), [cited 6 October 2014]. Available from the Internet: *www.frederickbuechner.com/content/touched-joy*.
3. John Ortberg, *The Me I Want to Be* (Grand Rapids: Zondervan, 2009), 242.
4. Eugene Peterson, *A Long Obedience in the Same Direction* (Downers Grove: IVP, 2000), 102.
5. Lewis Smedes, *Keeping Hope Alive: For a Tomorrow We Cannot Control* (Nashville: Thomas Nelson, 1998), 7.
6. N.T. Wright, *Surprised by Scripture* (New York: HarperOne, 2014), 61.
7. Ray Johnston, *The Hope Quotient* (Nashville: W Publishing, 2014), 14
8. Timothy Morgan, "Kay Warren: A Year of Grieving Dangerously," *Christianity Today* (online), 28 March 2014 [cited 6 October 2014]. Available from the Internet: *www.christianitytoday.com*.

.

LET'S BE FRIENDS!

VISIT OUR LIFEWAY WOMEN'S BLOG AT
lifeway.com/allaccess

LifeWay | Wome

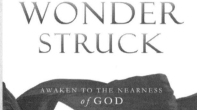

WONDERSTRUCK:
Awaken to the Nearness of God
7 sessions

Do you ever feel like you're going through the motions of faith? Sometimes we do and say the right things, but our hearts are far from God. We lose our sense of awe. But God says, "Therefore once more I will astound these people with wonder upon wonder" (Isaiah 29:14). The answer isn't more faith, greater obedience, or extra spiritual disciplines. God responds by giving us Himself. Join Margaret for this Bible study that will help you recognize the presence of God in the midst of your routine and discover joy in knowing you're wildly loved. *Wonderstruck* will remind you what it means to awaken to wonder—every day.

Member Book	005515743	$12.95
Leader Kit	005515840	$79.95

Contains DVD, Member Book with leader helps, and *Wonderstruck* book

SCOUTING THE DIVINE:
Searching for God in Wine, Wool, and Wild Honey
6 sessions

Explore how ancient livelihoods illuminate meaningful Christian truths that apply to life today through the eyes of a shepherdess in Oregon, a farmer in Nebraska, a beekeeper in Colorado, and a vintner in California. Gain new insight into biblical metaphors and discover answers to puzzling questions. Do sheep really know their shepherd's voice? How often does a grapevine need to be pruned? What does it mean for a land to be described as overflowing with honey?

Member Book	005258265	$9.95
Leader Kit	005189433	$74.95

Contains DVD, Member Book, Enhanced CD, and *Scouting the Divine* book

lifeway.com/margaretfeinberg | 800.458.2772 | LifeWay Christian Stores

Pricing and availability subject to change without notice.

LifeWay | Women

FIGHT BACK WITH JOY
SCRIPTURE MEMORIZATION CARDS

Scripture memorization is a spiritual discipline useful for filling our minds with what our hearts need. Psalms 119:11 (NIV) says, "I have hidden your word in my heart that I might not sin against you." When we memorize Scripture, it's easier to share the good news of Jesus, remain anchored in God's truth in difficult situations, and learn to meditate and delight in God's law (see Ps. 1:2).

If you're like me, memorization doesn't always come easily. When spending time disciplining myself in Scripture memorization, I have to think of mnemonic games or tricks to get each verse or passage to stick. I encourage you to do the same. Here are a few helpful hints that may assist you as you memorize each session's verses:

- Choose a translation that is easiest for you to remember or one you are most familiar with.

- Practice by writing out the verse three times. Each time begin writing without looking.

- Spend time dissecting the verse and meaning using the surrounding verses and a commentary. Scripture memory is easier when the passage is fully understood.

- Read the verse aloud three times, then try to recite it without looking.

- Use Google to see if any worship songs have been written about the passage you're memorizing or make up your own song to practice reciting.

- Find an accountability partner with whom you can recite verses together.

- Set a goal date to have a certain Scripture memorized.

- Write out the Scripture on colorful pieces of paper or paint on a canvas with your favorite Pinterest materials. Hang the artwork around your home or workplace to be reminded of the verse often.

- Write out the individual words on different note cards, mix them up, then try and put the words back in order.

- Be sure to break down the verse you're memorizing into smaller chunks to make it easier to swallow.

Don't get discouraged! Scripture memorization is a discipline which requires practice. I hope the flash cards will be something you carry with you throughout the next six weeks as you begin the process of memorizing.